# HARRY STACK SULLIVAN
*His Life and His Work*

*By the same author:*

MANAGEMENT OF EMOTIONAL DISORDERS, 1962

MANAGEMENT OF EMOTIONAL PROBLEMS OF CHILDREN
AND ADOLESCENTS, 1965, Second Edition, 1974

TEXTBOOK OF CLINICAL PSYCHIATRY, *An Interpersonal
Approach*, 1967, Second Edition, 1976

PUT-OFFS AND COME-ONS, 1968

SEXUAL MANEUVERS AND STRATAGEMS, 1969

THE PHYSICIAN'S GUIDE TO MANAGING EMOTIONAL
PROBLEMS, 1969

THE GAMES CHILDREN PLAY, 1972

THE INTERPERSONAL BASIS OF PSYCHIATRIC NURSING
(with Elza M. Almeida), 1972

MARITAL BRINKMANSHIP, 1974

IT'S ALL ARRANGED: *15 Hours in a Psychiatrist's
Life*, 1975

GROMCHIK, *And Other Tales from a Psychiatrist's
Casebook*, 1975

# HARRY STACK SULLIVAN

# SULLIVAN

*His Life and His Work*

by A. H. CHAPMAN, M.D.

*G. P. Putnam's Sons, New York*

SBN: 399-11734-2

Library of Congress Catalog
Card Number: 75-42926

PRINTED IN THE UNITED STATES OF AMERICA

# FOR JOSEPH SERONDE,

Emeritus Professor of Romance Languages,
Yale University,
who first instructed me in the evolution of ideas,
and for
Eric K. Chapman

# Contents

# HARRY STACK SULLIVAN
*His Life and His Work*

# *Preface*

MOST American psychiatrists, and many other behavioral scientists, now agree that the most original,
influential American-born psychiatrist was Harry
Stack Sullivan. He was the foremost developer of what
is known as the interpersonal approach to psychiatry.
He taught that the main field of study in psychiatry
and its allied disciplines should be the complex relationships between people; on the basis of interpersonal relationships he evolved his concepts of personality
development and emotional disorders. His impact on
American psychiatry and other behavioral sciences has
been extensive.

However, it is probable that most American psychiatrists and other behavioral scientists, including many
who have been much influenced by Sullivan's work,
could give only a limited outline of what he taught and
wrote, and the man himself remains more a legend
than a clearly understood figure. His ideas and treatment techniques have gradually, almost imperceptibly
permeated American psychiatry, and they are now being carried to a worldwide professional audience as
American concepts in psychiatry and social science

gain increasing acceptance outside the United States. Sullivan's influence is so pervasive, yet so unrecognized, that Leston Havens of the Harvard Medical School has said that he "almost secretly" dominates American psychiatry.

This unusual situation is owing to various factors. Sullivan was a homosexual, and this fact was known to, or strongly suspected by, most of his contemporaries. This has caused many people to absorb Sullivan's ideas and treatment techniques while acknowledging only partially, or not at all, their indebtedness to him. People who are strongly influenced by an artist, or a writer, or a scientist who is a known to be homosexual usually acknowledge their obligation to him; however, the "physician, heal thyself" concept, which is deeply embedded in the viewpoints of mental health professional workers, causes many psychiatrists and behavioral scientists to hesitate to admit their indebtedness to a psychiatrist whose homosexuality was commonly known.

Moreover, Sullivan during his lifetime exerted his influence more by his personal teaching and by word-of-mouth reports of his innovations in the treatment of patients than by his writings. Sullivan taught brilliantly, and by his treatment methods he set examples that were quickly copied and amplified by others, but he was a poor writer and he knew it. During his lifetime only one book of his teachings, containing five lectures he delivered as a memorial to his teacher and friend William Alanson White, was published, and this book was printed privately by Sullivan's colleagues and students against his inclinations; he later changed his ideas about many things expressed in that book. Sul-

livan wrote a moderate number of psychiatric articles, but they were printed in psychiatric and social science journals of relatively limited circulation. He rarely wrote for the general public and infrequently lectured to them, and he usually avoided giving interviews to the press and other media.

We today have a reasonable amount of Sullivan's mature thought in printed form only because during the last several years of his life a large number of seminars and lectures were recorded by his students and associates. This material was stored, and after his death in 1949 it was examined with the object of selecting parts of it for publication. The bulk of Sullivan's work now in print, and almost the only material that can be considered expressions of his fully developed viewpoints, is drawn from these recordings.

Sullivan, in contrast to many well-known psychiatrists, made no effort to make his life and work a monument to himself; he has become a distinguished figure almost in spite of himself. He viewed his teaching and writing merely as attempts to inform psychiatrists and members of the other behavioral science professions of ideas and treatment techniques which he felt were useful in understanding patients and giving them better care. At various times he also made limited attempts to adapt his ideas to social and cultural problems.

In addition, Sullivan's psychiatric career was relatively brief. Although he became a physician in 1917 at the age of twenty-five, he did not enter psychiatry until early 1922, when he was almost thirty years old, and he died twenty-seven years later in January, 1949. Though at times he held nominal medical school fac-

ulty appointments, he never primarily engaged in academic teaching, and with the exception of a short period early in his life he never held a research position. He spent his psychiatric career mainly in the treatment of patients and in personal supervision of other psychiatrists engaged in such treatment; he did his teaching and writing in time left over from this work. His current status in the history of psychiatry is an extraordinary tribute to the vitality and importance of his ideas and therapeutic innovations.

Sullivan's concepts are particularly relevant to the interpersonal and social dilemmas of our time. His emphases on healthy interpersonal relationships as the determinants of sound personality development and well-integrated social functioning are of special importance to a society in which families are disintegrating and in which people feel isolated, ill-at-ease and unsure of the purposes and meanings of their lives. His work also has implications for understanding the broader social problems, such as racial conflicts, generation gap estrangements and other difficulties which afflict us.

This book is intended for all persons who are interested in a better understanding of interpersonal relationships and their bearing on emotional health and social living. It should enable not only mental health professional workers who know little about Sullivan, but also many other college-educated or college-level readers to understand clearly what Sullivan thought and said. Desirably, this will help the reader in his daily appraisal of, and participation in, the many interpersonal relationships by which he continually evaluates himself and the people around him. To a large extent,

comfortable, successful interpersonal relationships are what life is all about.

In an attempt to make this book easily readable I have not encumbered it with footnotes and reference notes; such documentation, in my opinion, is more likely to discourage than enlighten the reader of a book whose object is to introduce him to an extensive body of thought. At the end of this book there is, instead, a selected list of the most important and readily available works of Sullivan, and each listing is followed by a description of the subjects it deals with and the ease or difficulty that may be expected in reading it. With this guide, interested readers may go on to explore selections of some of Sullivan's more accessible works.

The material of this book is drawn mainly from Sullivan's teachings during the last few years of his life. Throughout his career he often revised his ideas, and only the material of his last years can be accepted as his fully developed formulations; Sullivan made such extensive changes in his viewpoints, both in emphasis and content, that all material before 1943 must be considered preliminary versions. It took Sullivan twenty years of active work in psychiatry to arrive at his mature, final concepts.

A large measure of selectivity has necessarily been exercised in condensing Sullivan's work to an easily digestible, introductory volume. Also, a certain amount of interpretation has been essential in organizing the ideas of a man who wrote awkwardly and whose lectures and seminars, though impressive to those who heard them, are often rambling and obscure when printed.

A. H. CHAPMAN

15

# 1

## *The Life and Emotional Problems of Harry Stack Sullivan*

THROUGHOUT his life Harry Stack Sullivan struggled with emotional problems and difficulties in his relationships with people, which had marked effects on the psychiatric concepts he evolved. These problems prevented him from ever standing back and taking the attitude, "There is the patient, whom I, a sounder person with special insights, shall treat." His orientation was, "I, with my inescapable personality warps, and despite my emotional difficulties, shall work with this person to help him achieve better relationships with people and more emotional comfort. In the process both of us hopefully will grow and learn things."

Biographies of distinguished psychiatrists usually follow the theme "Behold the great man, and here is his message." This chapter, and this book, are not so written; they present the weaknesses, as well as the strengths, of both Sullivan and his work. Sullivan's problems contributed to his sensitivity, insight, and diligence in dealing with psychiatric patients. Because of his emotional difficulties, and his persistent awareness of them, he never fell into the error, so common among psychiatric innovators, of standing apart and

viewing patients as interesting specimens. For these reasons, Sullivan also could not elaborate fanciful abstract concepts, often expressed in diagrams, to speculate about what was going on inside patients. He always saw them as suffering individuals whose problems could not be portrayed in such artificial ways.

Some psychiatrists, including myself, feel that Sullivan's work makes him the most important figure in psychiatry in the last 100 years, and that his concepts and treatment techniques are much more valid and useful than those of Freud and many others.

Since this book aims to be no more than an introduction to Sullivan and his work, the various sources of information in the following biographical sketch will not be documented; such notations, as a rule, are of interest only to specialized scholars.*

## CHILDHOOD AND ADOLESCENT YEARS

Harry Stack Sullivan was born on February 21, 1892, in Norwich, New York, a small town which is

*Published biographical data on Sullivan includes the following: A detailed biographical vignette by Helen Swick Perry, Supplement 4 (December, 1974), *Dictionary of American Biography,* Charles Scribner's Sons, New York. Parts of *A History of the Washington Psychoanalytic Society,* by Douglas Noble and Donald L. Burnham, The Washington Psychoanalytic Society, Washington, D.C., 1969. Biographical sketch, *Current Biography,* H. W. Wilson Company, New York, 1942. The introductions and chapter commentaries of the 1962, 1964, and 1972 volumes of Sullivan's works listed in the Bibliography at the end of this book. The American Psychiatric Museum Association of Washington, D.C., and the William Alanson White Institute of Psychiatry, Psychoanalysis and Psychology of New York, have material on Sullivan. A biography of Sullivan by Helen Swick Perry is scheduled for publication by Basic Books, Inc., of New York.

the county seat of Chenango County. Norwich is set in an agricultural district about 200 miles northeast of New York City and a short distance above the Pennsylvania border. He was on both sides of Irish Catholic extraction. Although both his parents were born in the United States, all four of his grandparents had emigrated from Ireland during the famine following the failure of the potato crop in the late 1840's. His ancestors had long lived in the Irish Catholic counties of Clare and Cork. Out of this background Sullivan carried a slight Irish brogue which was noticeable by some people even when he was in his forties, and which became more marked when he was angry. This slight Irish accent is also evidence of his isolation from other children and adolescents during his developing years, for most of his childhood and all his adolescence were spent in non-Irish environments. Sullivan talked at times about his Irish extraction, though he had no strong opinions about the centuries-old political and religious problems of the Irish; even into the last years of his life he sometimes spoke of the Irish as "my people."

Sullivan's father was an emotionally withdrawn, distant man with whom Sullivan never had a close relationship; Sullivan in later years described him as "remarkably taciturn." His father occasionally praised Sullivan for his farm work and school accomplishments during his boyhood, but these rare comments did little to narrow the gulf between them. He remained a dim, vague figure on the periphery of Sullivan's emotional life. During the final years of his father's life, after the death of Sullivan's mother and when Sullivan had for many years been a physician, he got to know his father somewhat better on rare vis-

its back to his boyhood home, but this association merely gave Sullivan a clearer insight into his father's marked shyness and social ineptness.

The predominant figure in Sullivan's childhood home was his mother. Sullivan was an only child; his mother had two other children before him, but they died in early infancy. She was a continually complaining semi-invalid, and Sullivan bore the major brunt of her laments and unhappiness. She much resented the fact that in Ireland her family, the Stacks, had produced mainly educators, physicians, lawyers, priests, and other professional and middle-class people, but had sunk in social, educational, and economic status upon immigration to America. Morever, she felt that her social state had been further lowered, or at least had been made irreparable, by the failures of her husband, who never rose above the level of a factory worker and a poor farmer. Throughout his childhood she unloaded on her son her helpless anger, her tales of her family's former prominence, and impractical dreams of a better future. Sullivan many years later stated bitterly that he had escaped the problems of being an only child because his mother never took the trouble to notice the characteristics of her son, but used him as a coatrack on which to hang "an elaborate pattern of illusions."

Besides her accounts of the former prosperity and prominence of her family in Ireland, his mother told him myths of legendary ancestors. One of these myths related that an ancient ancestor of her family had been the West Wind, symbolized as a mystic horse which galloped constantly away from the rising sun to meet the future. One of Sullivan's most intimate friends in

later life, the psychoanalyst Clara Thompson, stated in her eulogy of Sullivan at his funeral services that, with his "sentimental, humorous Irish mind," she felt at times that he partially believed this myth. Sullivan in his adult years stated that the Irish were, in his opinion, the most pagan of civilized nations. He had a life-long fascination with horses and he used as his personal symbol a drawing of two horses' heads, one looking upward and one looking downward, enclosed in a circle; this emblem, which was partially derived from an ancient Chinese symbol for eternal life, appears on the title pages of his posthumously published books, and he used it in various ways during his lifetime.

At the time of Sullivan's birth his father was a laborer in a farm machinery factory in Norwich, and when Sullivan was three the family moved to a small farm, the property of his mother's family, near Smyrna, New York, about ten miles north of Norwich. Harry lived on this farm until he left Chenango County to go to college at the age of sixteen. On the farm he had no companions of his own age, and by the time he began grade school he was a socially awkward, shy boy. His clumsy efforts to get along with other children at school led to rebuffs and ridicule; he withdrew and became an outsider who never gained admission to childhood groups. He felt that his ostracism (this was the word he used in later years to designate such exclusion from childhood comradeship) was increased because the Sullivans were the only Catholic family in an old Yankee, Protestant farming community, and in the late nineteenth and early twentieth centuries there sometimes was anti-Catholic suspiciousness and prejudice in such settings. Although Sullivan in later

years stated that ethnic and religious differences were contributing factors to his isolation during childhood and adolescence, he probably overestimated their importance; the personality problems produced in his parental home were undoubtedly far more influential.

Sullivan received his grade school and high school education at the Smyrna Union School, a combined village grade and high school. He entered this school in 1897 or 1898, at the age of four and a half or five and a half. His early school records were destroyed in a fire, but his later school records still exist and show him to have been a superior student. His intelligence attracted the interest of the school's principal, an old friend of his mother's, and this teacher gave him special attention; for example, he occasionally took him on geological field trips in the surrounding region, and from him Sullivan learned rudimentary techniques of scientific observation. It was perhaps the kindness of this teacher, whom Sullivan remembered with special gratitude, which led Sullivan to decide to become a physicist if he could rise above his poverty and secure a university education. The only esteem Sullivan got throughout his childhood and early adolescence was achieved by scholastic excellence, but this did little to decrease his shyness and social ineptitude. He remained lonely, seclusive, and introspective.

When Sullivan was eight and a half he formed a close friendship, which probably lasted between two and four years, with a thirteen-year-old boy who lived on an adjacent farm. The five-year age difference between them was to have a marked effect on Sullivan's life course. Sullivan was hungry for someone to be close to, but the older boy was a sexually maturing

adolescent. Many years later Sullivan stated, both in lectures and in print, that when a close relationship is formed between a lonely child and an early adolescent of the same sex, homosexual exploitation of the younger partner usually occurs. (It must be emphasized, in this connection, that even Sullivan's most intimate friends knew virtually nothing of his childhood, adolescence, and early adulthood when, as a middle-aged psychiatrist, he said and wrote these things; his childhood history became known long after his death, when searches for biographical data on him were carried out.)

In his home community at the time it was generally felt that the relationship between Sullivan and the other boy was homosexual in the full genital sense of the word. Evidence of the homosexual nature of this relationship is also found in a manuscript Sullivan wrote between 1929 and 1933, to which he gave the odd title *Personal Psychopathology*. In this manuscrpt, for example, Sullivan states that a close friendship between a boy of eight and a half (he specifies that age) and a sexually maturing adolescent almost invariably becomes genitally homosexual. This book, which is clearly autobiographical in parts, was published twenty-three years after Sullivan's death. Neither Sullivan nor the other boy ever achieved a heterosexual pattern of adjustment, and neither married. Strangely, both these boys became psychiatrists, though their viewpoints on the nature and treatment of psychiatric illnesses differed much; the other individual spent his psychiatric career in various units of a large state psychiatric hospital system and died three years after Sullivan's death.

## College, Medical School, and First Professional Experiences

At sixteen Sullivan graduated from high school; he was the top student in his class and its valedictorian. On the basis of his school record and his grades on the New York State Regents examinations, he won a state scholarship to Cornell; at sixteen and a half, in the fall of 1908, he for the first time left his home community to attend Cornell at Ithaca, New York.

At Cornell he was enrolled under his full baptismal name, Harry Francis Stack Sullivan, and began a science course with the intention of becoming a physicist. In his first year he took chemistry, physics, mathematics, and mechanical drawing. At the end of the first term his grades were above average, but during the second term they fell markedly; in June of 1909 he was suspended for failure in all his subjects.

During this second term of college some kind of disaster occurred in Sullivan's personal life; its nature is not clear. According to rumors in his home community, he was apprehended in some type of misdemeanor with a group of older boys and feigned mental instability to avoid the legal consequences of his actions. However, his scholastic failure and suspension from college may have a simpler explanation. He was an emotionally immature, socially awkward, adolescent farmboy, away from home for the first time, and he may simply have found the demands of a major Ivy League university beyond his emotional and scholastic stamina; moreover, failure in the one area of his life in which he had found any self-esteem, his studies, could have caused him much emotional turmoil in

*24*

his final period at Cornell and for some time afterward. The rumors of legal difficulties and mental illness, feigned or actual, may have been unfounded. Nevertheless, after this failure Sullivan never returned to his home community in Chenango County, except for brief visits.

The fact that his Cornell records state that he could return to study there at a later date would seem to contradict the rumors that he was involved in any kind of scandalous behavior. According to his school records, he was "dropped for failure to do satisfactory work," and nothing else; there is no other verifiable information about his leaving Cornell. I inquired by mail circular to the remaining members of his Cornell class (there were 239 of them alive at the time of inquiry) if any of them could remember Sullivan and could give information about the circumstances of his suspension, but without results. Sullivan probably lost his scholarship at Cornell because of his scholastic failure, and his consequent financial destitution is sufficient to explain his inability to continue his education there or at any other undergraduate college. Since no efforts were made to collect biographical data on Sullivan until many years after his death, much information about the first three decades of his life has been permanently lost.

Some persons who knew Sullivan during the last twenty years of his life, and some commentators on his work, have speculated that during his late adolescence he had a psychiatric illness; some of these persons have specified that he may at this time have had a brief schizophrenic illness. The evidence for this is vague and contradictory. In his later life Sullivan told a few

people that in his early years he had been psychiatrically hospitalized for a short time. However, Sullivan unfortunately was sometimes dishonest in talking about events of the first three decades of his life. He concealed many things and invented others to fill the gaps. For example, not even his most intimate friends ever knew that he had attended Cornell; he said that he went directly from high school to medical school, and the truth was discovered many years after his death by interviewing elderly distant relatives in Chenango County. Sullivan in later years at times hinted that he had special insights into schizophrenia because of some kind of personal experience with it during his late adolescence, but careful study of available data leads to the unpleasant suspicion that he may have concocted stories about psychiatric illness and psychiatric hospitalization in order to justify his claims that he had special sensitivity in working with schizophrenics. He never specified where, when, or under whose care he was ever psychiatrically treated. He did not mention any psychiatric illnesses on applications for military service, government positions, and medical school in after years.

Also, between 1909 and 1915 he earned enough money to enter medical school and work his way through it despite marked poverty, and to stand all the economic and emotional hardships involved; it is difficult to believe that a recently schizophrenic person could do this at a time when there was no specific treatment for this illness and its prognosis was grim in the vast majority of cases. It is conceivable that Sullivan was briefly hospitalized for a lesser kind of late adolescent emotional turmoil, but there is no verifiable evidence even for this.

This question is further complicated by the eccentric manner in which Sullivan used the term "schizophrenia." He defined schizophrenia as a state of panic accompanied by some degree of interpersonal incapacity. He employed the terms "paranoid transformation" and "hebrephenic deterioration" for the conditions which most psychiatrists, both then and now, call schizophrenia; he said that these states were "two untoward outcomes of schizophrenic illnesses," rather than true schizophrenia. Sullivan unfortunately used the term "schizophrenia" so vaguely in his later years that it could be applied to any kind of emotional disturbance in which the individual had strong anxiety, even of brief duration.

Sullivan's fiasco at Cornell and his failure to attend any other undergraduate college had profound effects on his intellectual development. As will be outlined later, because of his lack of a college education, he could gain admittance to only a shabby, run-for-profit medical school in Chicago which in later years he described as a "diploma mill." At this school instruction was rudimentary and graduation depended on the payment of tuition rather than scholastic performance. Hence, Sullivan never had any type of sound formal education after his year at Cornell.

His college failure had other long-term detrimental consequences. Sullivan never learned to write easily comprehensible English, and to organize his thoughts well on paper; he probably would have learned these things to a reasonable extent during a four-year education at an outstanding university such as Cornell and during attendance at a good medical school. He also did not acquire the skills usually gained in laboratory work in the physical and biological sciences, and as a

result his concepts of scientific methods and research were poor until he was approaching middle age. In addition, the gaps in his knowledge of basic physical and biological sciences, general medical subjects, and broad cultural fields are at times flabbergasting to the informed reader of his writings and published lectures and seminars. His terminology, as well as his literary style, has a clumsiness that smacks of years of solitary, unguided self-instruction. Sullivan never acquired facility in using similes and metaphors to explain his ideas, and his works are devoid of the occasional references to literature, art, music, mythology, and history which give color and grace to psychiatric writing; in all these things Freud, Jung, and various others excelled. On many cultural subjects Sullivan was all his life a relatively ignorant man.

Sullivan spent the next thirty-five years of his life struggling to overcome these educational deficiencies, and only in his writings and lectures after the age of fifty do we at times find facility in expressing his thoughts and organizing them. The emotional consequences of his poor education were probably as marked as the intellectual ones; they probably contributed much to his tendency to camouflage the shoddiness of his early life with fabrications and exaggerations.

However, his lack of education had some advantages. Though he did not acquire the skills which an adequate education would have given him, he also did not absorb the set attitudes, subtle prejudices, and conforming ideas which a standard education often instills. When, almost by accident, he entered psychiatry at the age of thirty, he was free of the ingrained points

of view which usually direct a beginning psychiatrist's thinking along one of the customary paths. If Sullivan had had a standard education he probably would have been an outstanding psychiatrist, but it is doubtful that he would have made his original, revolutionary contributions to psychiatry. This, of course, is no basis for arguing against adequate formal education for professional people; as Bagehot long ago pointed out in another context, success in a lottery is no argument for lotteries.

Sullivan left Cornell in June, 1909, at the age of seventeen, and nothing is known of his whereabouts and activities until the summer of 1911 when he was in Chicago applying for admission to medical school there. Whether he suffered much emotional turmoil in his final months at Cornell and needed time to recuperate, or whether he could not face returning as a college failure to his home community and therefore worked at various jobs in the Midwest, is not known, and probably never will be. It is most likely that he worked during this two-year period to get the money to begin medical school.

Why did Sullivan choose medicine after his failure in studying physics? In later years he simply stated that his interests shifted from physics to medicine, and gave no reasons for the change. He also said that one of his physics professors commented that in this change the field of physics had suffered a marked loss. This is, to say the least, an odd statement about a student who made no outstanding grades during the first term of his freshman year of studies in physics and failed all subjects in his second term. Sullivan also said in later years that he entered medical school because of a

strong interest in psychiatry. However, as will be discussed later, there is no evidence that Sullivan had a special interest in psychiatry until a job assignment with the Veterans Bureau accidentally brought him into administrative contact with psychiatric patients in 1922, when he was almost thirty years old and had been out of medical school for five years. The most likely explanation is that he entered medical school since it was at that time the only kind of scientifically oriented professional education open to a person who had no more than a high school diploma. In 1911 there were in the United States hundreds of proprietary, shabby medical schools which accepted students who had only a high school education. Such education, tawdry as it was, would enable Sullivan to obtain professional status in a scientific field.

In September, 1911, Sullivan entered the Chicago College of Medicine and Surgery, which had been founded ten years previously. It occupied an old building in a poor section of Chicago and had no clinic or hospital affiliations. Between 1880 and 1910 thirty-one medical schools of this type were founded in Chicago, many of them lasting only long enough to collect fees from a few classes of students. One physician, Dr. Johann Malok, obtained charters for six separate medical schools during a two-year period. The lax laws which allowed these schools to be chartered and to graduate poorly trained physicians were gradually reformed following the 1910 publication of the Flexner Report on American medical education, and the state licensure laws which permitted their graduates to be licensed were in time revised. The medical school which Sullivan attended became extinct in 1917, the

year in which he got his degree; this school, along with four similar ones, was purchased by Loyola University School of Medicine as part of a general plan to close down inferior medical institutions.

Sullivan's grades in medical school were slightly above average, but it is difficult to evaluate them in a commercial medical school of this kind. Sullivan in later life stated that, with the exception of the instruction received from two or three teachers, he got his medical education by solitary study, and supplemented it with subsequent paid work in a Chicago hospital and in the medical departments of several Chicago factories and business organizations. However, this work's primary aim was earning money. Sullivan lived in poverty during his medical school years and spent most of his time working to make money to support himself and pay medical school fees. He taught elementary physics, worked as a conductor on the Chicago elevated railway, and had other kinds of employment. Little more than this is known reliably about Sullivan's life during medical school.

Sullivan finished his medical school studies in 1915, but because he owed money to the school for back tuition and fees the school refused to give him his diploma until these debts were paid. Hence, during the next two years Sullivan did various kinds of medical work in the Chicago area to pay off this indebtedness. He worked as plant physician for the Illinois Steel Company in South Chicago and Gary, Indiana, and worked in some capacity at the West Side Hospital in Chicago. He did medical examinations for insurance companies; in 1942 he described himself in print as the "medical director for the Western departments of five

casualty insurance companies" in early 1917; this could hardly have been accurate since he had not yet received his medical school diploma.

By September, 1917, Sullivan paid off his debts and the medical school in that month gave him his diploma. However, the school was operated in so careless a fashion that no notation of his graduation was made in any of the school's records. Long after Sullivan's death, when biographical inquiries began, proof of his graduation was established only by discovery of his medical school diploma among his personal papers. On his medical school records (which passed into the archives of Loyola School of Medicine) he is consistently listed as Harry F. Sullivan, but his diploma is made out to Harry Stack Sullivan.

In the seven-year period between 1915, when he finished his medical school studies, and early 1922 when, almost by chance, he was brought into contact with psychiatric patients in his work as a liaison officer between the Veterans Bureau and St. Elizabeths Hospital in Washington, D.C., Sullivan had a checkered career. The available records about his Chicago employment in industrial medicine, military service during World War I, and postwar federal government jobs in which he dealt with disabled veterans, contain much conflicting data on places, dates, and activities; even so elementary a fact as Sullivan's date of birth varies by as much as six years from one record to the next, and the biographical data which Sullivan himself gave in later years about his activities during this period are not consistent.

It seems clear, however, that until September, 1917 Sullivan spent most of his time in various kinds of in-

dustrial medical work (which he could do on the basis of having completed his medical studies, even though he had not yet received his diploma) in the Chicago area. In 1916 he was mobilized briefly as a member of the National Guard and served in a military unit patrolling the Mexican border during the disturbances there. In 1918 he was licensed to practice medicine in the State of Illinois, and during the same year was appointed a first lieutenant in the Army; he served as junior member of a medical examining board throughout the war. In April, 1919, after leaving the Army, he took a job in Chicago as assistant district medical officer in the Division of Rehabilitation of the Federal Board of Vocational Education; this involved general medical work with men disabled during the war. He became medical executive officer of this government unit in late 1919. In August, 1921, this agency was merged with two other government bureaus dealing with ex-servicemen into a new agency, the Veterans Bureau, which in later years became the Veterans Administration.

Sullivan continued working in the Veterans Bureau until November, 1921, when he was given a newly created position as liaison officer representing the Veterans Bureau at St. Elizabeths Hospital in Washington, D.C. Sullivan apparently had spent a short time in Washington doing administrative medical work regarding disabled veterans prior to November, 1921; however, most of his work in these government agencies was done in the Chicago area. There was a break in his government service in late 1921 when he went back to Smyrna, New York, to care for his father during a severe illness. He afterward returned to Chicago,

where he was informed by telegram of his appointment as liaison officer at St. Elizabeths; however, it seems that he did not take up his duties at St. Elizabeths until early 1922. He remained at St. Elizabeths until October of the same year.

Although Sullivan later made occasional statements to the contrary, there is no sound evidence that he specifically dealt with psychiatric problems of disabled veterans during the years of his government employment until he reached St. Elizabeths. It seems probable that he dealt with all types of physical and psychiatric disabilities of ex-servicemen; however, a sizable minority of such difficulties are usually neurological and psychiatric. In a 1942 biographical sketch based on data which he supplied, Sullivan specified 1922 as the year in which he entered psychiatry.

The appointment to St. Elizabeths was a turning point in Sullivan's career. Many psychiatrically disabled veterans were hospitalized at St. Elizabeths, a large federal government psychiatric hospital that accepted patients referred to it by various government agencies. The Veterans Bureau needed a physician at St. Elizabeths to act in a liaison capacity between itself and the hospital. Sullivan did not apply for this position; it was offered to him on the basis of his former government service in Chicago and Washington.

When Sullivan began his work at St. Elizabeths he was almost thirty years old. Until this time there is no reliable evidence that he had a particular inclination to work in psychiatry, as opposed to any other medical specialty. Though in after years Sullivan dated his interest in psychiatry to various times before 1922, careful examination of the facts does not support this, and

in the last year of his life he stated that his entrance into psychiatry occurred "accidentally" (his word) when he received his appointment to St. Elizabeths.

The evidence that he had no previous special interest in psychiatry is varied. In later years he stated that during both his medical school course and his military service his talents and interests were in internal medicine. During medical school he made the lowest passing grades (D's) in psychiatry and neurology, though his grades in general were average or above. If he had had a strong inclination to work in psychiatry before 1922 he could, from 1915 onward, have worked at one of more of the many small private psychiatric hospitals in the Chicago area to make the money he needed to pay off his medical school debts; there were at that time many such hospitals and they had chronic shortages of staff, but he chose other kinds of work. He did not seek employment in any special psychiatric capacity for about three years after discharge from the Army, but did general medical work for various government agencies dealing with disabled veterans. During these years he could easily have worked in private or state psychiatric hospitals. Also, he could have gone into psychiatric residency training in Chicago or elsewhere, there being a constant demand for candidates for residencies in psychiatry since it was not a popular medical specialty at the time.

There are two further points that should be covered before leaving this general period of Sullivan's life. In later years he stated on various occasions that in the winter of 1916–1917 he had seventy-five hours of psychoanalysis in Chicago. However, impartial examination of the facts suggests that at best Sullivan's

statement was a misleading exaggeration and at worst a fabrication. The first psychoanalyst did not arrive in Chicago until 1921, and there was no activity that could be called psychoanalytic in Chicago in 1916 and 1917. It is possible, of course, that Sullivan had some kind of counseling or interview treatment by a self-trained person, and that he later chose to dignify this with the name of psychoanalysis, but even this is clouded by doubt since Sullivan refused, even in the last years of his life, to name the person who gave him this treatment and to discuss any aspects of it. Some of his close colleagues during the 1920's and 1930's suspected that he had no psychoanalysis until he had it with Clara Thompson in New York in 1933.

What could Sullivan's motive have been in inventing this tale? In the psychiatric environment at St. Elizabeths Hospital, and in the general Washington-Baltimore psychiatric community of the 1920's and early 1930's, Freudian psychoanalysis was the dominant mode of thought, and to play the role that Sullivan assumed in these circles he had to have as part of his credentials at least minimal personal therapeutic experience with psychoanalysis; it was a professional necessity.

The second point to be noted about this period of Sullivan's life is that he never had any formal training in psychiatry; he never took a residency in psychiatry or had any other kind of systematic education in it. He merely went to work in it in 1922. He got his knowledge of psychiatry by working with patients and by attending lectures, seminars, and case discussions in the Washington-Baltimore area during the early and middle 1920's. Good psychiatric residency training was easily available and had long been well developed in

the Washington-Baltimore region, New York, and many other cities at that time. Of course, the opportunities for psychiatric self-education in the stimulating atmosphere of St. Elizabeths were excellent, but Sullivan entered this situation as a staff physician, not as a student.

His lack of systematic training in psychiatry had many unfortunate results. Throughout his life his knowledge of depressive psychoses, manic illnesses, organic brain syndromes, and many other psychiatric disorders was strikingly defective. He often used psychiatric terminology in such inaccurate, eccentric ways that an unwary reader of his works may be badly misled or altogether baffled. Even in the last years of his life he at times employed psychiatric terms that had already become outdated when he entered psychiatry.

However, Sullivan's lack of formal psychiatric education had certain advantages. He did not adopt the ideas of any particular school of psychiatric thought. He did not acquire the prejudices that extensive formal training would probably have instilled in him, and which might later have hindered him in evolving his own unique system of psychiatry. In the 1920's he paid lip service, at least in his writings and public addresses, to the new, modish Freudian concepts, but this was a passing phase in his psychiatric development.

By default, Sullivan learned psychiatry from the most reliable of teachers, the patients. He was fascinated by the patients he saw on the wards of St. Elizabeths, especially the schizophrenics, and this absorption remained with him for the rest of his life.

Sullivan had another important source of psychiat-

ric education—his own personality problems, which dogged him all his life. He was acutely aware of the ways in which his early emotional traumas had made him inept in many interpersonal areas, and his homosexual urges jabbed him intermittently until his final disease-ridden years.

Guided by the patients who gripped his attention, and goaded by his own emotional difficulties, Sullivan spent the next twenty years developing his special approach to psychiatry; in the last half dozen years of his life he recorded it in the lectures and seminars from which his posthumously published books were constructed.

## SULLIVAN'S EARLY YEARS IN PSYCHIATRY: WASHINGTON AND BALTIMORE

When Sullivan arrived at St. Elizabeths he for the first time came into contact with a first-class medical and intellectual environment, and it made a profound impression on him. He was particularly fortunate in the type of psychiatric atmosphere which he encountered there. It was dominated by William Alanson White, a brilliant, experienced, charming psychiatrist of international reputation, who had a comprehensive knowledge of psychiatry and wrote and taught well. Although White was one of Freud's earliest exponents in the United States, he had strong reservations about many of Freud's concepts and felt they should be accepted only with modifications. White made no enduring, original contributions to psychiatric thought, but he molded a number of persons who did so. He has

been called "the great encourager." He took special interest in Sullivan and directed his early steps in psychiatry; he also treated Sullivan with a kindness and respect that no one had ever given him. In return, Sullivan conceived for White an admiration and veneration he never felt for anyone else.

The psychiatric climate at St. Elizabeths under White was stimulating; a group of able psychiatrists were experimenting with new ideas and new methods of dealing with psychiatric patients. Though there was much interest in the ideas of Freud, Jung, Sandor Ferenczi, and Adler, all points of view were accepted under White's tolerant leadership. The Washington Psychoanalytic Society had been organized at St. Elizabeths under White and his colleagues in 1914. This was a society for the discussion of the ideas of Freud and other psychoanalysts rather than systematic training in psychoanalytic points of view; at its regular meetings papers were presented, case histories were examined, and general discussions ensued. In 1913 the first psychoanalytic journal in English, the *Psychoanalytic Review,* had been started by White and his associates at St. Elizabeths, using their own money to fund it. White's textbook of psychiatry, which was first published in 1907 and went through fourteen editions by 1935, included a wide variety of psychiatric viewpoints.

There also was considerable interchange between St. Elizabeths and the department of psychiatry at Johns Hopkins Medical School in nearby Baltimore, which was under the leadership of Adolf Meyer. Meyer was Swiss-born and Swiss-educated, but he spent his entire professional career in the United States and

from 1910 to 1941 was head of the department of psychiatry at Johns Hopkins. Meyer had a profound effect on American psychiatry and, as Sullivan himself often stated, a marked influence on the development of Sullivan's ideas. Since direct associations between the two men were limited, Meyer's impact on Sullivan was mainly by his writings and his general influence in the Washington-Baltimore area.

Meyer, more than any other person, was responsible for focusing the attention of American psychiatry on the emotional and interpersonal causes of psychiatric illnesses; this was in strong contrast with the prevailing Continental European concept that most forms of psychiatric illnesses were caused by physical disorders of the brain, whose biochemical or chromosomal natures would in later years be discovered. Since the first decade of the twentieth century Meyer had been teaching, first at Cornell University Medical School and then at Johns Hopkins, that most psychiatric disturbances, including schizophrenia, the manic-depressive psychoses, and the neuroses, were caused by emotional stresses and unhealthy relationships with close people in the patients' lives. Simple as this concept sounds today, it was revolutionary in its time; although he was aware of Freud's ideas Meyer developed his psychiatric concepts independently, and his ideas differ markedly from those of Freud.

Meyer's position as professor of psychiatry at Johns Hopkins, then the leading American medical school, gave his opinions much influence. For thirty years Meyer trained at Johns Hopkins many men who later became the heads of psychiatric departments in America's major medical schools, and his influence in En-

gland also was marked. To a large extent, the widespread interest in Freudian psychoanalysis in America is owing to the fact that Meyer prepared the way for an emotionally oriented system of psychiatric thought. Throughout his life Sullivan acknowledged his debt to Meyer's ideas.

During his year at St. Elizabeths Sullivan threw himself enthusiastically into work with patients; apparently his administrative duties as liaison officer between the hospital and the Veterans Bureau absorbed only a small part of his time. He was especially interested in the emotional problems of the young male schizophrenics who formed a large part of the Veterans Bureau's psychiatric population at St. Elizabeths. Sullivan spent much time talking with them and he supplemented his clinical work with wide-ranging reading on psychiatry. In this work and reading he was guided by White, but White allowed him to proceed in whatever direction his interests led him.

Although Sullivan read much and was influenced by many writers, he acknowledged a special debt to the clinical work and thinking of Edward J. Kempf, a long-forgotten psychiatrist who worked intensively with schizophrenic patients at St. Elizabeths from 1914 to 1920, after prior training at Johns Hopkins under Meyer. By the time Sullivan arrived at St. Elizabeths Kempf had moved to New York to enter private practice, but he had recorded his general ideas and his experiences with patients in a 1921 book titled *Psychopathology*. This 762-page book was not successful; it was little read and did not go into a second printing. This is owing to Kempf's rambling literary style and the unpopularity at that time of much of his subject

matter—the psychology of patients with schizophrenia and other psychoses. However, probably on William Alanson White's suggestion (Kempf's book was dedicated to White), Sullivan read this book and it strongly impressed him; in Kempf's book one can see the crude origins of some of Sullivan's basic ideas about personality development and the causes of psychiatric illnesses. Sullivan was careful in later years to point out the influence Kempf had on him.

In 1923, probably based on recommendations from William Alanson White, Sullivan moved from St. Elizabeths Hospital to the Sheppard and Enoch Pratt Hospital, a well-known private psychiatric hospital in a suburb of nearby Baltimore. Sullivan took a position as one of the staff psychiatrists at Sheppard Pratt and remained there until 1930. Under the tolerant, able leadership of Sheppard Pratt's director, Ross McClure Chapman, Sullivan during these years underwent an important phase of his development as a psychiatrist. By his choice, Sullivan worked mainly with young male schizophrenics. He found that he did not work well with female patients. They apparently made him uncomfortable at this time; he admitted both in lectures and in print his inability to work well with female patients until later in his career. During his seven and a half years at Sheppard Pratt Sullivan became a nationally known psychiatrist because of his studies of schizophrenics and his innovations in treating them.

Once launched into psychiatry Sullivan rapidly became prominent. His energy and dedication in working with patients, and in writing about his work, brought him quickly to the fore of American psychi-

atry. He presented his first paper to a national psychiatric meeting in 1924, and published two or three papers each year after that for the rest of the decade. These papers dealt almost entirely with schizophrenia, the most common psychotic illness; at that time half the patients in American psychiatric hospitals were schizophrenics. He delivered papers on schizophrenia in several American cities, and in 1926 became an associate editor of *The American Journal of Psychiatry,* a position he held until 1939. For three issues in 1928 he was acting editor-in-chief of this journal, the foremost psychiatric periodical in the United States. During the 1920's he wrote twenty-seven book reviews for this journal; his reviews were carefully done and, although wordy, superior to the general quality of book reviews in the periodical. During the 1920's Sullivan was active, both as a member and as an officer, in various psychiatric societies in the Washington-Baltimore area.

In 1924 he was appointed an instructor in psychiatry at the University of Maryland Medical School in Baltimore, and from 1925 until 1930 held the title of associate professor of psychiatry in that school; however, his duties probably did not involve more than once- or twice-weekly lectures to medical students at various times during the academic year. With the exception of a brief period in 1939, when he was professor of psychiatry and interim director of the department of psychiatry at Georgetown University School of Medicine in Washington, D.C., this was the only academic position Sullivan ever held.

Except for a few anecdotes of doubtful reliability, there is little information on Sullivan's personality

characteristics, life-style, and relationships with his colleagues and friends at this time. This type of information is available only from about 1930 onward.

During the 1920's Sullivan paid lip service to Freudian-psychoanalytic theories in the papers he wrote and presented at psychiatric meetings, and was generally accepted in Washington and Baltimore as a Freudian. However, careful examination of his papers and of his then unpublished manuscript *Personal Psychopathology*, which he wrote between 1929 and 1933, reveals that almost from the beginning his thinking had strong non-Freudian features. In addition to the ideas of William Alanson White, Adolf Meyer, and Edward Kempf, Sullivan was influenced by the concepts of many psychiatrists and social scientists (some of whom are now little known) such as T. V. Moore, W. H. R. Rivers, William McDougal, David Levy, Edward Sapir, Charles H. Cooley, G. H. Mead, Bronislaw Malinowski, and others. However, the system of thought which Sullivan eventually matured by the early 1940's cannot be traced to any single predecessor or group of predecessors; it was uniquely his own.

In the 1920's Sullivan worked mainly with schizophrenics, with whom Freudian psychoanalysts had had little experience, and since it was readily admitted that on-the-couch psychoanalytic techniques could not be applied to most schizophrenics and other psychotic patients, Sullivan was able to live in professional harmony with his Freudian colleagues. He held elected administrative positions in psychoanalytic societies in the 1920's and early 1930's. However, as the 1930's proceeded it became apparent to his contemporaries that he was developing a system of psychiatric

thought that was sharply opposed to almost all the basic tenets of Freudian psychoanalysis. As this became clear bitter quarrels, both at public psychiatric meetings and in smaller groups, between Sullivan and the Freudians began, and they lasted until the end of his life.

In 1925 Ross McClure Chapman, recognizing Sullivan's talents, created for him at the Sheppard and Enoch Pratt Hospital a new position, director of clinical research. Sullivan had no special grants of money, but he was given a free hand in using hospital space, facilities, personnel, and patients in whatever way he wished. In early 1929 Sullivan set up at Sheppard Pratt the special ward for treating schizophrenics which was to make him a prominent figure in American, and later world, psychiatry. What he did seems commonplace now, but when he did it it was a striking innovation.

Sullivan organized a six-bed ward that was run as a separate unit in the hospital. The six patients who occupied this ward were at all times young male schizophrenics. Sullivan reasoned that if the patient became sick because of unhealthy interpersonal relationships (he had begun to use the term "interpersonal relationships" in 1927) they would improve if they lived in an environment in which they had healthy interpersonal relationships tailored to meet their needs. This was the first time anyone tried to implement this concept.

Sullivan carefully selected six male aides, four for the day shift and two for the night shift, and he intensively instructed them on how to talk and act with the patients. His aim was for the entire staff to form comfortable interpersonal relationships with the patients

to help them come back from the psychotic worlds into which they had retired; in the process the patients would develop capacities for sounder relationships with people and would gradually acquire better contact with reality. Sullivan held daily meetings with the aides to discuss what each of the patients did and said, and he outlined how each faltering step of the patients to reach out to other people could be encouraged.

In doing this, Sullivan·used techniques that were novel, varied, and ingenious. For example, he thought that many of these young male schizophrenics had much inner turmoil about brief homosexual urges or actual homosexual episodes during adolescence; Sullivan therefore trained the aides to discuss how they too had experienced such feelings briefly during adolescence, and perhaps had had occasional episodes of homosexual play with other boys (such as mutual masturbation) in late childhood. The aides emphasized to the patients that such feelings and experiences should not be guilt-laden and devastating, but were simply aspects of the wide-ranging kinds of things people did at certain times in their development. Also, many kinds of recreational activities uniting the patients and aides in a well-integrated social group were organized.

In addition, Sullivan himself held daily interviews with the patients, often with one of the aides present in the room to give it a group atmosphere. In these interviews he dealt with the patient's past and current feelings, activities, and experiences on whatever level the patient could talk. He had extraordinary understanding of schizophrenics and remarkable patience with them. In later years he often demonstrated his capacity

to engage quickly in a give-and-take dialogue a schizophrenic with whom other psychiatrists had for days or weeks been unable to establish contact. His tolerance of patients' upset behavior was also noteworthy. On one occasion a very disturbed patient struck him; Sullivan smiled slightly and asked, "Feeling better now?"

At the end of a year the results of treatment on Sullivan's ward were examined, and it was found that his schizophrenics had done much better than schizophrenics with similar clinical conditions did. About 80 percent of them had improved, and at that time this was a remarkable improvement rate. From the viewpoint of today's research methods, however, it is difficult to assess these results. Sullivan worked with a relatively small number of patients, and he chose them out of the general schizophrenic population of the entire Sheppard Pratt Hospital. Also, much hinges on Sullivan's use of the term "social recovery." Most of his patients did not recover entirely; they still had evidences of schizophrenic processes. However they were able to make better adjustments at home, or in a permissively run psychiatric ward, than schizophrenics who were treated by the conventional methods then employed; also they were able to relate to people much better than schizophrenics who had not had the therapeutic experience he had given them. Nevertheless, we do not know what happened to these patients in the long run; we do not know what were their states at two-year, five-year, and ten-year intervals following this treatment. The patients whom Sullivan picked for his ward were quite sick schizophrenics, for at this time he used the conventional criteria for schizophrenia and not the less distinct criteria he employed in lat-

er years; this is clear from case reports he published in psychiatric journals in the 1920's.

Sullivan described his results with a frankness and objectivity that was rare for psychiatric innovators of his day; in evaluating his treatment results he was, for example, much more discriminating and franker than Freud was. Nevertheless, the true revolution in the treatment of schizophrenia, with dramatic improvement of its prognosis, was to come twenty-five years later, in the early and middle 1950's, when the phenothiazine antipsychotic medications were developed. The modern treatment of schizophrenia usually consists of the administration of phenothiazine antipsychotic medications to patients in psychiatric wards run along the general lines of Sullivan's model ward.

However, Sullivan had developed and put into practice a new concept of psychiatric hospital care, and had showed that it helped patients significantly. The main therapeutic emphasis in this treatment, moreover, was not on exploration of the patient's past life in detailed interviews, as in Freudian psychoanalysis, but on providing a sound interpersonal environment in which healthy interactions with the hospital staff gradually corrected unhealthy patterns of feeling and thinking.

The theoretical, as well as practical, implications of this kind of treatment in time had a profound effect on American psychiatry. It raised the following question: Should psychotherapy be carried out by Freudian-psychoanalytic free associational methods, or should psychotherapy consist of a much more flexible type of dialogue between a psychiatrist, as an expert in interp-

ersonal relationships and emotional problems, and a patient who had warped patterns of relating to people? Sullivan's eventual answer to this question, in his final formulations during the middle and late 1940's, established his system of interpersonal psychiatry.

Sullivan's ward became famous in American psychiatric circles, and in time its reputation spread beyond the United States. Sullivan described its operation in a few addresses to psychiatric meetings and in articles he published in psychiatric journals. However, word-of-mouth reports of it were much more important in the spread of this new concept of psychiatric treatment and the theoretical questions it raised. By the early 1930's Sullivan may fairly be described as one of America's best-known psychiatrists.

Of Sullivan's personal life during the 1920's little is known with certainty. When, long after his death, biographical searches about Sullivan's life began, the people who could have given extensive information about him were dead, or their memories were dulled by time and age. A few things about him, however, can be verified. In 1927 he adopted a fifteen-year-old boy, a former patient, as his son. This boy, James, took Sullivan's surname and remained with him for the rest of Sullivan's life. In later years he acted in a secretarial capacity to Sullivan, and ran his household. Sullivan always was careless about his personal papers, his financial affairs, and his housekeeping arrangements, and James took over many duties which freed Sullivan for concentration on his professional work.

We do, however, know a good deal about Sullivan's private thinking on psychiatry and his feelings on

many other subjects during the 1920's, including a great deal he never revealed publicly. These things are recorded in the manuscript of a book he wrote between 1929 and 1933, and never published. Owing to his abrupt death in Europe in 1949, and the confused state of his personal papers, this manuscript was not destroyed. During the early 1930's he had used fragments of it at seminars and conferences, but by the middle 1930's he had decided firmly against ever publishing it. Twenty-three years after his death, and much against the wishes of some of his friends and colleagues, this manuscript was published as a book, bearing the odd title which Sullivan had given it in 1929, *Personal Psychopathology*.

As a record of Sullivan's early psychiatric thinking, and of his struggles to come to grips with his own emotional problems, this book, begun when he had been working in psychiatry for only seven years, has value for biographers of Sullivan who are tracing the slow, painful evolution of his ideas. However, it does not represent Sullivan's mature formulations. This book should never have been published, but since it has, we must examine it.

The book is so disorganized and badly written that in some sections it is difficult to see what the author is driving at. He uses archaic words in eccentric ways, and he sometimes detours into aimless diatribes. This book shows Sullivan as a passionate, immature, emotionally confused person. It reveals his homosexuality, and it discloses weird concepts and prejudices. For example, he states that a prolonged period of active genital homosexuality during late childhood and the first

part of adolescence is essential if a person is to have sound mental health, in both adolescence and adulthood. If an individual does not have this long period of genital homosexual experience, Sullivan writes, he will probably become a schizophrenic and be socially and mentally incapacitated for the rest of his life; such homosexual experience may also protect the person against other types of psychiatric disorders. He also says that this long genital homosexual phase is imperative for the later development of sound heterosexual capacities. In a gruesome footnote Sullivan makes a strong plea for the death penalty for anyone caught persuading an adolescent or young adult to experiment with opium-derived narcotics. Much of the final chapter of this book is an incomprehensible tirade. It is pointless to discuss further the contents of this painful book. Perhaps Sullivan wrote it, at least in part, as a self-therapeutic procedure; he soon afterward saw the folly of publishing it, and those of his contemporary colleagues to whom he showed it agreed.

Nevertheless, examination of this manuscript gives important information for evaluating Sullivan's life work. It demonstrates clearly that Sullivan spent a long time maturing, both as a person and as a psychiatrist, and that his psychiatric concepts were much influenced by his personal anguish and traumatic life experiences. Parts of the book are virtually autobiographical. The emotional tumult expressed in this book emphasizes that Sullivan could never stand off and theorize in impersonal, mechanical ways about patients. He felt a kinship with psychiatric patients which, coupled with twenty-seven years of studying

them, enabled him to come closer than anyone else has yet come to understanding the nature of psychiatric illness.


## THE NEW YORK PERIOD

About the middle of 1930 Sullivan decided to go into private outpatient practice in New York City. Until that time his entire psychiatric experience had been with hospitalized patients, mainly schizophrenics; he had had little contact with neurotic patients and persons with character disorders. It is probable that he also had financial and other motives for making this move. His reputation preceded him to New York, and in early 1931, when he opened his office, he quickly became established. During his eight years in New York he had a large, lucrative practice.

During his period in New York Sullivan had 300 hours of personal psychoanalysis under his friend and colleague Clara Thompson. However, this psychoanalytic treatment was not conducted along classical Freudian lines. In 1927 Sullivan met Clara Thompson at a psychiatric meeting at Johns Hopkins Medical School, where Thompson was then in psychiatric residency training. They became good friends. In the winter of 1927-1928 the Hungarian psychoanalyst Sandor Ferenczi spent much time in the Baltimore area, giving lectures and conducting seminars. Although Ferenczi had been one of Freud's earliest disciples and had long been a close friend of Freud, he had markedly diverged from Freud in both theory and treatment techniques. Ferenczi's divergences from Freud may,

52

with oversimplification, be summarized as follows: He advocated a much more flexible kind of psychotherapy than on-the-couch psychoanalysis by a relatively inactive analyst. He proposed that effective psychotherapy often required an active role by the therapist in a vibrant give-and-take dialogue and interaction with the patient. Ferenczi's point of view was therefore in harmony with Sullivan's evolving concepts of interpersonal relationships both as the causes of psychiatric problems and as the major tools for treating them.

Feeling that Ferenczi was on a more valid course than Freud, Sullivan in 1930 urged Clara Thompson to go to Europe for extensive psychoanalytic training under Ferenczi; Thompson had had brief therapy from Ferenczi in the summers of 1928 and 1929. Thompson accepted Sullivan's advice, and between 1931 and 1933 she was psychoanalyzed by Ferenczi in Budapest. In 1933 her therapy by Ferenczi was ended by his death; at the time of his death Ferenczi was virtually ostracized by Freud and his followers because of his marked departure from Freudian principles.

After Clara Thompson's return to New York in 1933 Sullivan had about 300 hours of psychoanalysis by her, and this was Sullivan's only verifiable psychoanalytic treatment. However, Clara Thompson in later years said that they stopped the analysis after 300 hours because she had such awe of Sullivan's intellectual capacities that she could not effectively go on with it. This statement suggests that this was not a typical kind of psychoanalytic experience.

During his 1931 to 1939 period in New York Sullivan continued, by twice-monthly trips, to be active in psychiatric activities in Washington and Baltimore.

He attended psychiatric meetings, delivered papers, and participated in professional organizations in both cities. In 1933 he played a major role in the formation of the William Alanson White Foundation in Washington and in 1936 of the Washington School of Psychiatry. The school was designed to be the teaching agency of the William Alanson White Foundation, and Sullivan was the head of its division of psychiatry. The William Alanson White Foundation included other kinds of behavioral and social scientists, and Sullivan's close friend Edward Sapir, an anthropologist and linguist, was head of its division of social sciences.

The William Alanson White Foundation was set up to receive and use philanthropic funds for psychiatric teaching and research. A few years after its inception, and especially after the death of William Alanson White in 1937, a long series of clashes, both of personality and psychiatric points of view, began among Sullivan and others who were active in it. By the late 1930's this foundation, which operated teaching branches in both Washington and New York, had become dominated by Sullivan, and until his death he used the White Foundation and the Washington School of Psychiatry as outlets for the expression of his evolving viewpoints.

In 1938 the journal *Psychiatry* was founded by the William Alanson White Foundation, with Sullivan as one of its editors. After several years of bitter disagreements among Sullivan and the journal's other editors and its publication committee, Sullivan became its sole editor and employed it for publishing his articles, editorials, and lectures. The journal published articles

by many psychiatrists and social scientists, but in time these articles tended to conform to Sullivan's interpersonal concepts. Through the William Alanson White Foundation, the Washington School of Psychiatry, and the journal *Psychiatry*, Sullivan's ideas reached an increasing audience of psychiatrists, psychologists, psychiatric social workers, and behavioral and social scientists during the late 1930's and the 1940's.

During the 1930's Sullivan's abandonment of Freudian-psychoanalytic principles became steadily more apparent to his colleagues, though he still retained his memberships in psychoanalytic societies. Bitter quarrels between Sullivan and the Freudians began to occur at psychiatric conferences and public meetings, and they continued for the rest of Sullivan's life. The ferocity and crudeness which occurs at times in psychiatrists' quarrels would shock many laymen. Nasty squabbling frequently contaminated Sullivan's speaking at both professional meetings and teaching conferences. From the middle 1930's onward Sullivan was much sought out by other psychiatrists for instruction in small groups and individual supervision of cases they were treating. In all professional contexts Sullivan's angry comments, sarcasm, and scorching criticism of colleagues and students became legendary.

From the middle 1930's onward Sullivan had continually less patience with psychiatrists and behavioral scientists who advocated Freudian theories and rejected his own interpersonal concepts. At times, however, his irritability had a more reasonable basis. He was always the patient's advocate, and obvious insensitivity by a psychiatrist to a patient's problems, or

tendencies to theorize about patients rather than to understand their suffering, brought tongue-lashings from Sullivan. It made no difference whether the offender was a distinguished psychiatrist presenting a paper before a full auditorium or a psychiatric resident in a small teaching conference.

Sullivan knew that his temper outbursts were often unreasonable; he admitted to close friends that, because of his childhood and adolescent isolation, he never developed good capacities for give-and-take cooperation and compromise. Because of his vicious attacks on both the theories and personalities of his colleagues, feelings about Sullivan in New York, Washington, and Baltimore became sharply polarized. He was hated by many and admired by some. Sullivan usually won his verbal battles, but impartial examination of the records of some of these professional meetings indicates that on many occasions his opponents chose to abandon the field rather than to descend to Sullivan's level of rudeness and insult. Sullivan's adherents called him witty and brilliant; his opponents, who in time became more numerous, found him crude and vituperative.

During the 1940's Sullivan became progressively more isolated professionally, but he remained all his life the dominant person in the William Alanson White Foundation, the Washington School of Psychiatry, and the journal *Psychiatry.* Although his estrangement from various psychiatric circles in Washington, Baltimore, and New York became ever wider, he always had a dedicated group of friends and supporters.

We have much information about Sullivan's life in the 1930's and 1940's. During his years in New York

he lived in an old brownstone house on East 64th Street, which he bought when he moved there, and in which he also had an office. When he arrived in New York in 1931 his finances were in a characteristically chaotic state, and he borrowed two thousand dollars from the New York psychoanalyst Abraham A. Brill to make the down payment on the house. Sullivan was financially generous to the point of imprudence; he gave much money to friends, and at times to patients. When anyone expressed apprehension about accepting sizable sums from him Sullivan waved the objections aside saying, "There is always more."

He opened his New York house to whoever of his colleagues and friends needed a place to live. The people who at times lived in Sullivan's house included Erich Fromm, who was to become a distinguished psychoanalytic writer, Philip Sapir, the son of Sullivan's old friend Edward Sapir, Patrick Mullahy, a young Irishman who was to become a noted commentator on Sullivan's theories, Katharine Dunham, the black dancer who was a former patient of Sullivan's, and many others. Sullivan had a large income from his clinical practice and also from the fees paid by other psychiatrists for supervision of their treatment cases by him. He stated that he was one of the four or five best-paid psychiatrists in New York at the time, and this may well be true. As a rule Sullivan was gentle and loyal to his friends, but even with long-term friends he occasionally could be abruptly angry; however, he often went out of his way to heal such hurts later.

Beginning in the late 1920's and extending throughout his life Sullivan had much interest in the social

57

sciences; he felt that there should be much cross-fertilization between psychiatry and sociology, anthropology, social psychology, and linguistics. The interpersonal theories which he was evolving in psychiatry dovetailed well with various sociological and anthropological concepts. Some of Sullivan's close friends, with whom he sometimes collaborated in conferences and in writing papers, were sociologists, anthropologists, and linguists. Sullivan frequently stressed that many changes should be made in society to create an environment which would be emotionally healthier for all its members.

However, Sullivan's impact on the social sciences has been much overestimated by some of his interpreters. If the contemporary fields of sociology, anthropology, social psychology, and other social sciences are carefully examined, relatively little evidence of Sullivan's influence is found. He made no basic contributions to these fields, and his efforts to weave psychiatric and social science concepts together were superficial and unsuccessful. Sullivan's true influence has been on psychiatry and its allied mental health fields such as clinical psychology, psychiatric social work, psychiatric nursing, and psychiatric hospital administration. The final chapter of this book examines ways in which Sullivan's ideas can be employed in solving social dilemmas, but this is an extrapolation of Sullivan's work; he himself made only limited steps in this direction.

There are still alive a fair number of Sullivan's colleagues, students, and friends who can give information about his physical appearance and general lifestyle during the 1930's and 1940's. Although he was

about five feet ten inches tall and of average frame, he usually gave the impression of slight build. He was balding in front and combed his hair backward. In young adulthood he had had a full mustache, but in the middle 1920's he narrowed it to a thinline mustache which he wore for the rest of his life. From early adulthood onward he wore metal-rimmed, yellow-tinted glasses; some people described his gray-green eyes as dark and penetrating, and found them the most striking part of his features. He tended not to look directly at a person with whom he was talking, but looked away from his companion at about a 90-degree angle, glancing up only occasionally. He attributed this mannerism to his many years of working with schizophrenics; at various times in his lectures he reported that he looked away from schizophrenic patients since he found that a steady gaze made them uncomfortable. However, it is probable that this sideward looking habit was caused mainly by his shyness and social awkwardness.

At social functions and with close friends Sullivan could be gracious, and even charming, in conversation and manner, and when the subject did not deal with some aspect of psychiatry he rarely lost his temper or harshly criticized others. He dressed well but not foppishly, but this was to a large extent owing to the attention which his son gave to his wardrobe. He liked martinis, made with vodka and mixed with unsweetened grapefruit juice, before dinner, and enjoyed brandy after dinner. Though occasionally he drank more than was prudent, alcohol was never a problem for him, despite contentions of some of his critics to the contrary.

Sullivan had much interest in the problems of the

blacks. He had close friendships with a few black social scientists, and in the middle 1930's he frequently entertained officials of the National Association for the Advancement of Colored People (NAACP) at his New York home. In 1937 and 1938 he spent brief periods doing research on the special emotional problems of black adolescents and young adults in Washington, D.C., and he made a short field trip to Nashville, Tennessee, in connection with this work. He felt keenly that grave injustices were done to the blacks. Charles S. Johnson, president of Fisk University and a black friend of Sullivan's from the middle 1930's onward, gave one of the eulogies at Sullivan's funeral services.

Sullivan was very loyal to his close friends, and with them he was almost always gentle and considerate. The following anecdote is characteristic. On one occasion Sullivan's adopted son left a glass two-piece coffee maker on the stove to answer a telephone call from a patient, and when he returned the coffee maker had boiled over and was broken. Sullivan, observing the mess, lost his temper and berated him. Two days later Sullivan sent his son out on a small errand. When he returned he found Sullivan standing at the kitchen door, apparently chagrined and sheepish. When his son asked what the trouble was, Sullivan replied with seeming embarrassment that during his son's absence he had broken a new, similar coffee maker in the same way. It was Sullivan's way of healing the hurt he had given.


## THE RETURN TO WASHINGTON

By the late 1930's Sullivan had achieved his objec-

tive of gaining experience in the outpatient study and treatment of patients with neuroses and personality disorders; he thus had balanced his previous work with hospitalized psychotics. During the 1930's he also had much experience in teaching, both in lectures and in supervising psychiatric trainees in the treatment of their difficult or perplexing cases. In 1938 he decided to move back to the Washington-Baltimore area, and during late 1938 and early 1939 he made this move.

He bought a house on an acre and a half of land in Bethesda, Maryland, just outside Washington, and lived there for the rest of his life. He laid out its gardens and personally worked in them, though most of the labor was done by a part-time gardener; he was particularly interested in raising day lilies. He kept several cocker spaniels and bred them. Sullivan liked fine music, though his understanding of it was limited. He built a multispeaker sound system on which he enjoyed listening to Mozart, Wagner, Beethoven, Brahms, and other classical composers; Mozart was his favorite. He had an office in his home, and he also did much of his case supervision work with psychiatric trainees there. His son, by then a man in his late twenties and early thirties, ran the household, helped him manage his financial affairs, and did some of his personal secretarial work.

However, despite his busy professional life in Washington and Baltimore and his twice-monthly trips to New York for teaching and case supervision work at the New York division of the William Alanson White Foundation, Sullivan remained a lonely man. His mother had died in 1926 and his father in 1931, and after their deaths his contacts with relatives in

Chenango County, which were never close, virtually ceased. His family life included only his adopted son and himself.

Moreover, between Sullivan and even his closest friends there was always a gap. For example, none of them knew about his year at Cornell, nor what he did during the two years after it; in fact, no one knew more than a few facts about his life until he arrived at St. Elizabeths in 1922 at the age of almost thirty. He carried no friendships, and only a few distant acquaintanceships, from the first three decades of his life into the last twenty-seven years of it. Most of the people who knew him in the middle 1940's had first met him less than fifteen years before then. Despite admirers, professional associates, and a constantly growing reputation, there was always an atmosphere of isolation in Sullivan's life, and he felt it keenly. There were, of course, the added problems of his sexual life. By his own admission, he never achieved a genital heterosexual relationship, and he felt this was a painful failure. Despite the discretion he exercised in his homosexual contacts, some of his close friends knew of his sexual difficulties, and in professional circles his homosexuality was generally suspected. Further discussion of Sullivan's sexual life would harm the families of persons recently dead.

In 1939 the William Alanson White Foundation decided that a series of lectures should be given to honor the memory of White, who had died in 1937, and Sullivan was chosen to give them. He gave five lectures to small audiences in an auditorium in a building of the Department of the Interior, lent for this purpose. In these lectures Sullivan made his first public attempt to

present comprehensively his ideas on personality development, psychiatric disorders, and psychiatric treatment. These lectures were published in the February, 1940, issue of *Psychiatry*, at the urging of Sullivan's associates and students, and in response to many requests for copies of them. Sullivan felt that in these lectures he had expressed his ideas inadequately, but he agreed to their publication. They attracted much attention in psychiatric and social science circles, and in the following years many mental health and social science professsional workers wrote to secure copies of this issue of the journal, and the available supply of reprints became exhausted.

In 1947, much against Sullivan's inclinations (he said he had changed his views on much of the material, and that the first three lectures, in particular, were "grossly inadequate"), a new printing of these lectures was made by *Psychiatry*, and the copies were encased in hard covers. This book carried the title Sullivan had used for the lecture series, *Conceptions of Modern Psychiatry*, and this was the only time during Sullivan's lifetime when his viewpoints appeared in book form. During the next several years 13,000 copies of this book were sold by the William Alanson White Foundation through *Psychiatry*, almost entirely on the basis of write-in requests. This remarkable publishing record, which to a large extent occurred on the basis of word-of-mouth reports, indicates the widespread demand that existed for information on Sullivan's ideas. Under the same title this book was published commercially four years after Sullivan's death and still sells well each year, though many of its ideas are not in accord with Sullivan's final, mature views.

When the United States began its military buildup in 1940, Sullivan published through the William Alanson White Foundation a memorandum on psychiatric criteria for the selection of military personnel, and in that year he was appointed psychiatric adviser to the national headquarters of the Selective Service System in Washington. He quickly became de facto head of its psychiatric division. Sullivan was a patriot. He dropped his lucrative practice and case supervision work, and for more than a year, in 1940 and 1941, devoted himself full-time at negligible pay to work with the Selective Service System. He wrote directives and bulletins, gained personal experience by doing psychiatric examinations in local Selective Service facilities, and traveled, largely at his own expense, to hold seminars in many cities throughout the nation for psychiatrists and other physicians who were doing psychiatric examinations of military selectees.

Sullivan emphasized that such examinations should be done with reasonable care so that men who were likely to break down psychiatrically during service would be excluded. He pointed out that if such care were not taken, poorly selected men would become psychiatric casualties during service and would undergo much avoidable suffering; he also warned prophetically that they would subsequently become long-term medical and financial burdens on the government.

Sullivan's insistence on reasonably careful examinations brought him eventually into conflict with General Lewis B. Hershey, who as head of the Selective Service System wanted a quick buildup of the military services and was skeptical about the psychiatric problems which Sullivan predicted. Sullivan resigned from his position as adviser to the Selective Service System,

but later events proved him farsighted. Throughout the war he acted as occasional psychiatric consultant to the military services; he was one of the first persons to be informed, at a special session convened at the Aberdeen Proving Ground, of the development of the atomic bomb.

## SULLIVAN'S FINAL YEARS AND THE MATURE FORMULATION OF HIS IDEAS

Sullivan's most creative period began after he resigned from the Selective Service System and returned to his clinical practice, teaching activities, and case supervision work in the Washington-Baltimore area in late 1941. From the winter of 1943-1944 onward he each year gave a series of lectures outlining his views on personality development, psychiatric disorders, and psychiatric treatment, in his capacity as the leading figure of the William Alanson White Foundation and the Washington School of Psychiatry. Almost all these lectures were recorded, and the recordings were preserved. Also, from October, 1942, to April, 1946, he gave a total of 246 teaching seminars at Chestnut Lodge, a well-known private psychiatric hospital in Rockville, Maryland, a suburb of Washington. All these teaching sessions were similarly recorded. Sullivan, now in his fifties and with more than two decades of psychiatric experience, was ready to formulate his fully developed views, and he did so in these lectures and seminars. With the exception of editorials for *Psychiatry* and a few other pieces, he wrote relatively little after 1942.

It is in these recorded lectures and seminars be-

tween 1943 and his death in January, 1949, that his true contributions are found in their final form. After his death his friends and colleagues set up a fund for selecting the best of this material and publishing it in a set of three books. These books are *The Interpersonal Theory of Psychiatry* (1953), *The Psychiatric Interview* (1954), and *Clinical Studies in Psychiatry* (1956).

The last few years of Sullivan's life were spoiled by ill health. He was nursed by his son and close friends through four serious cardiac illnesses. He preferred to be treated at home, and his friends brought to his house the medical equipment he would have had in a hospital. During one episode of subacute bacterial endocarditis (a bacterial infection of the inner lining and valves of the heart) his friends saved his life by securing a large amount of penicillin, which was then difficult to obtain.

Also, his final years were embittered by an ever-widening separation in the Washington-Baltimore psychiatric community between a large group composed of Freudians and a small group who accepted the non-Freudian interpersonal viewpoints of Sullivan. This separation further increased Sullivan's loneliness and isolation.

After the end of the Second World War Sullivan saw the dangers of a return to the former national and ideological rivalries between nations in a world equipped with atomic weapons and increasingly complex armaments. He therefore devoted a significant part of his time to organizing and participating in conferences, both in America and Europe, under the auspices of the World Health Organization and the United Nations, to seek ways for decreasing international tensions and

avoiding war. He felt that his viewpoints on interpersonal relationships could contribute to improving relations between nations. He outlined at conferences and in a few articles his ideas about ways in which nations could break down the barriers that separated them. In retrospect his plans seem naïvely idealistic, but Sullivan at least saw the dangers long before most national leaders and the general public in the West realized them.

In early January, 1949, he went to Amsterdam to attend an executive meeting of the World Federation of Mental Health, which was to make plans for organizing cultural interchanges to reduce international tensions. Impatient with the complacent, bureaucratic atmosphere of the meeting, Sullivan verbally flailed some of his fellow conferees. The meeting ended without concrete plans. Discouraged about the prospects for international understanding along the lines h⸍ was advocating, Sullivan traveled to Paris on his way home. There, on January 14, he died of a brain hemorrhage in his hotel room, alone.

His body, after a brief delay, was cremated, and his ashes were returned to America. On the morning of February 11, in accordance with his previously expressed wishes, his ashes were buried with Catholic and military ceremonies in Arlington National Cemetery, across the Potomac from Washington, D.C. Although he had abandoned the practice of the Catholic religion in middle adolescence, he always respected the order and beauty of its traditional rites. His headstone bears a simple cross, under which are his name, his rank as a captain in the medical reserve from New York State in World War I, and the dates of his birth

and death. On the evening of the day of his interment a memorial service was held in the Sternberg Auditorium of the Walter Reed General Hospital in Washington, during which eulogies were delivered by several of his friends and professional associates.

# 2

## Sullivan's Concepts of Interpersonal Relationships

### Personality: Its Nature and Characteristics

Personality, Sullivan states, *consists of the characteristic ways in which a person deals with other people in his interpersonal relationships.*

Thus, if a person as a rule insists on having his way in his relationships with his marital partner, friends, and work associates, and either cajoles or bullies them to get it, one of his personality characteristics is that he is domineering. If, on the other hand, he in most instances lets other people control him, one of his personality characteristcs is that he is passive. In each case a personality characteristic is defined on the basis of things which other people can *see, hear,* and sometimes *feel* in their relationships with this individual. His family and friends can *see* and *hear* him as he deals with them in a domineering or a passive manner, and they can *feel* their own reactions of resentment, or disgust, or pleasure as he treats them in dominant or passive ways.

A psychiatrist, a clinical psychologist, a psychiatric nurse, or some other mental health professional work-

er can also see, hear, and feel this individual's domineering or passive personality characteristics. A mental health professional worker can get such information in three ways. He can talk with this person to find out what goes on in his life and how he gets along with people. The therapist can also note whether this person tends to be controlling or passive in the interpersonal relationship that gradually develops between the two of them. In some instances the therapist can also interview the person's marital partner, adolescent children, and others with whom he has close relationships.

A domineering or passive tendency is, of course, only one of many facets of a personality structure, and no individual is completely domineering or passive in all his interactions all the time. We are here discussing an isolated personality feature in a simple way for ease in illustrating a general principle.

*Sullivan builds his approach to psychiatry on the study of personality characteristics which can be directly observed in the context of interpersonal relationships.* Although at first glance this approach may seem simple, or even obvious, it is crucial in understanding Sullivan's thinking.

Almost all other systems of psychiatry are based on statements about things alleged to be occurring in the patient's "mind." Various psychiatric systems use terms such as "psyche," "integrated central nervous system," and "psychobiological organization" but these terms usually mean more or less the same thing as "mind" when they are carefully examined. The fundamental problem with all these systems of psychiatry is that things going on in the "mind" *cannot* be *seen, heard,* and *felt.* Being unobserved and unobservable,

the things said to go on in the "mind" can never be more than vague speculations; they can be neither proved nor disproved. They are beyond the reach of scientific investigation. A statement which cannot be proved or disproved must forever remain a matter of faith, or opinion, or prejudice.

Systems of psychiatry based on statements about what is going on in the patient's mind are therefore similar to a system of thought which is built on axioms such as "All events are controlled by Divine Providence." The truth or falseness of this statement cannot be established by things that reasonably well educated people can *see, hear,* and *feel.* Much human experience can be cited to support such a statement, and much human experience can be cited to nullify it, but it is so set up that it must always remain a matter of faith.

This basic point can be illustrated by an example from clinical psychiatry. For ease of exposition the case will be presented in a simplified manner.

A sixteen-year-old boy huddles in a corner of his bedroom. He whispers that he does not want to leave the room because of fears that people outside his room want to harm him. The pupils of his eyes are dilated in terror, his hands tremble as he reaches for a glass of water, and he is mute most of the time. How do we describe and explain this boy's state?

A person employing Sullivan's interpersonal approach to psychiatry would say that the boy is in a state of panic and is withdrawing from people because he finds contacts with them painful and threatening. Because of, and as part of, his loss of contact with people he is developing delusional ideas. If a therapist, or the members of a psychiatric hospital staff try to help

this boy, their job is to bridge the interpersonal gap between him and them. They thus help him to return to sounder contacts with people and with the broad spectrum of things we call "reality." If a detailed case study is carried out it probably will be learned that he suffered damaging interpersonal relationships during childhood and early adolescence, and upon facing interpersonal stresses in middle adolescence he deteriorated into his present condition. We can *see, hear,* and *feel* these things. We are therefore on sound observational, scientific ground.

A therapist who evaluates this boy from a Freudian-psychoanalytic point of view sees him differently. He says that this boy's ego structure has crumbled, or at least is functioning in a grossly defective manner, because instinctual forces and repressed conflicts from his id are assailing it. He perhaps would add that the ego is being further impaired by pressures from his superego. As a result of these conflicts the patient is flooded with panic. In addition, the patient has much internal hostility and other emotional forces, perhaps of a sexual nature, which he is projecting from himself onto others. He thus avoids feeling that he is hostile toward other people, which he would find painful to realize, and instead feels that others are hostile toward him; he feels that they are so hostile that they wish to harm him. Hence he huddles in terror in the corner of his room.

All things in this Freudian-psychoanalytic explanation *cannot* be verified by anything that anyone can *see, hear,* or *feel.* No one has ever seen, or will see, an id, an ego, or a superego; there is no way that their characteristics can be verified or measured, or that their exis-

tence can be proved. Also, no one has ever seen a person cast hostility out of himself and attach it to others. These concepts are similar to the proposition that "all events are controlled by Divine Providence." They must forever remain matters of speculation or faith.

Freudian-psychoanalytic statements about this boy may contain elements of truth, just as myths, legends, and popular beliefs may contain elements of truth. They also may have practical usefulness is working with patients; as philosophical speculations they may give therapists an ideological framework for helping people. However, the unprovable nature of Freudian doctrines makes them treacherous. Anyone using them is free to elaborate new speculations about what is going on in this boy's "mind," and these new speculations also can be neither proved nor disproved. This, of course, is what has occurred endlessly in psychoanalysis as Jung, Adler, Rank, Reich, Klein, Horney, and many others have set up divergent schools of psychoanalytic thought, each claiming true insight and that all others are false.

Freudian psychoanalysis has been used in this example since most readers are more likely to be somewhat familiar with it than with other systems of psychiatric thinking; almost all other schools of psychiatry could have been similarly used.

If the interpersonal approach offers the only objectively verifiable method for studying emotional disorders, and alone has the possibility of becoming in time a truly scientific system, why don't all psychiatrists and mental health professionals adhere to it?

Other systems of psychiatric thought may be unproved and unprovable, but they offer therapists, and

73

others, comforting, complete explanations of everything in psychiatry. For example, when working with a patient, the therapist has, in moments of perplexity and stress, a completely worked out, dogmatic system to rely on. It tells him what to do in any situation and explains anything that went wrong. If a patient commits suicide, or becomes worse, or fails to improve despite prolonged therapy, the therapist is spared the pain of uncertainty. In brief, other systems give therapists what they *need*, emotionally and intellectually.

Sullivan's interpersonal approach, on the other hand, offers a psychiatrist no such comforting system. As this book will outline, the interpersonal approach emphasizes that the emotional problems of no two people are exactly alike. Moreover, it stresses that information about a patient is always to a certain extent distorted by being *seen, heard,* and *felt* by the therapist; that is, the therapist, by virtue of being human, is an imperfect observer. In treatment of patients the interpersonal approach demands continual agility and flexibility from the therapist; in many situations it gives him a point of view, but no guidelines. Sullivan repeatedly stated that in psychiatric treatment one person, who is designated an expert in interpersonal relationships, is using his inescapably imperfect personality to aid another person, designated the patient, who comes for help with his unique problems in feeling, thinking, and relating to people.

Most other psychiatric systems provide the therapist with a format that both physically and intellectually buffers him from the patient. For example, the classical Freudian therapist sits out of sight of the patient and remains silent most of the time; maintaining the

flow of talk is the patient's responsibility. In contrast, the interpersonal approach throws the therapist into a pit with the patient and says: "With the utmost flexibility that you can muster, you must engage in a vibrant give-and-take dialogue with the patient. The direction of this dialogue is unpredictable. There are no sure guidelines, but only general principles, and human difficulties are too variable to allow dogmatic generalizations." Sullivan said there was no fun in psychotherapy, and that it was the hardest kind of work he knew.

When he defined personality, and based his approach to psychiatry on the basis of interpersonal relationships, Sullivan understood clearly what he was doing. He emphasized that this approach alone offered hope that one day psychiatry would become a truly scientific discipline. Although he occasionally strayed from this principle, as when, during the 1930's, he speculated about something he called the "self," he usually realized in time that he had deviated from his own principles. When he laid down his fully developed views in the last few years of his life, most of his thinking was consistent with his basic standards.

### THE FORMATION OF PERSONALITY

*Personality is formed by the interpersonal relationships an individual has, especially with close persons, during his entire lifetime.* The most intensive phase of personality development begins in infancy and extends through early adolescence; it continues in a significant manner during middle and late adolescence

into early adulthood, but personality never becomes a fixed, rigid thing. A person of sixty interacts with people differently from the way he did when he was twenty; though he may carry various tendencies and general patterns from early adulthood onward, these tendencies and patterns are modified continually by the changing interpersonal relationships and social circumstances of his life. An adult's characteristic ways of interacting with people—that is, his personality—are affected by whether his marriage is satisfactory or miserable, by whether or not he has children, by whether his career is is going well or badly, by whether he is living in poverty or comfort, and by many other things.

There is, however, a certain tendency for the personality structure which a person has developed by middle to late adolescence to persist in its broad, general outlines. A self-centered, domineering person of twenty tends to be self-centered and domineering at the age of sixty; however, marked changes in his personality may occur, depending on what happens interpersonally to him in the intervening forty years.

The interpersonal approach emphasizes more than most other psychiatric systems the effects on personality of the society and culture in which an individual is reared and lives. A Chinese, an Australian tribesman, and a Chicagoan have quite different ways of interacting with people, and hence different personality characteristics, which to a large extent are determined by their cultures. In addition, ongoing social changes affect personality; if Chinese society becomes urbanized and industrialized, if a nomadic Australian tribe settles in a stable agricultural community, or if a Chicago neighborhood become violence-ridden and vice-

infested, the personalities of the involved people are often affected.

The ways in which a personality feature is formed in the context of interpersonal relationships may be shown in the following example, which is much simplified for purposes of illustration.

Throughout his developing years a boy is reared by a passive mother who permits him to dominate her, and by a professionally busy father who spends little time with him. During childhood he is allowed to bully his younger sister and to manipulate his mother by temper tantrums, and he does the same things by angry tirades when he is an adolescent. In his neighborhood associations he continues this pattern by asssociating only with children whom he can control in similar but subtler ways. At school he sulks, and occasionally rebels, when teachers reprimand him, and he at no point in childhood and adolescence has close interpersonal relationships in which he develops capacities for harmonious give-and-take on an equal basis with other people. In middle and late adolescence he tends to associate mainly with a small circle of persons whom he can govern. He can camouflage this personality trait for brief periods when it is necessary or prudent, as in classrooms and other social situations, but his aggressiveness quickly emerges when such restraints are removed.

Depending on many factors, this boy may in adulthood become an aggressive businessman who stamps roughshod over his associates but is successful because of his talents, or an alcoholic who daily assuages the turmoil within himself as his domineering qualities cause him vocational, marital, and social failures. Depending on a wide variety of interpersonal, eco-

nomic, social, and physical health variables, this man may be a controlling but affectionate husband of a passive, dependent wife, or an angry, desolate misfit who goes through a series of unhappy marriages leaving a train of emotionally damaged children behind him. As the result of many, largely unpredictable variables, he may at some point cease to be in the group of those persons whom we call healthy and may enter the group of those whom we call sick. *The health or sickness of his personality—that is, the characteristic ways in which he deals with other people in his interpersonal relationships*—is dependent on his constantly changing physical, social, and interpersonal environment as well as on his past and current life experiences. An individual has innumerable such characteristics, and the totality of them forms his general personality, the individual whom we know.

To readers who are accustomed to more intricate theories of personality structure these principles may seem overly simple; indeed, they may seem commonsensical and obvious. The fundamental principles of all valid systems of thought, from Darwin's theory of evolution to Einstein's theory of relativity, are simple when they are clearly explained. It is necessary to understand thoroughly these fundamentals in order to comprehend easily the more complex features of Sullivan's approach to psychiatry.


## ANXIETY

Anxiety is one of the central concepts of interpersonal psychiatry. Sullivan employs this term in a special

way. *By anxiety he means virtually all basic types of emotional suffering; thus anxiety includes anxiousness, guilt, shame, dread, feelings of personal worthlessness, eerie loathing, and other less definable painful feelings.* Anxiety varies in degree from mild discomfort that is scarcely noticeable to disorganizing, incapacitating panic.

It perhaps would have been better if Sullivan had employed a different term to designate so broad a spectrum of painful feelings, for in other systems of psychiatry, as well as in popular usage, anxiety has a narrower meaning. Broader terms such as anguish, or emotional pain, or emotional distress would have conveyed at first glance more accurate concepts of what he meant. However, Sullivan uses the word "anxiety" so often and so basically that any attempt to substitute another term for it is now infeasible.

Anxiety can be detected and described in various ways. A person who has it can outline how he feels. He can describe his apprehensiveness, anxiousness, dread, guilt, shame, eerie loathing, feelings of worthlessness, and other distressing feelings. Astute interviewing often is required to determine the nature and degree of the person's emotional suffering, and to understand how he feels and perceives it.

In its more marked forms anxiety often can be directly observed. The anxious person's physical restlessness, apprehensive glances, sweat-glistening palms, facial muscular tenseness, tremulous hands, and other signs of inner turmoil can be noted. The agitation and disorganized behavior of a panicky person may be immediately obvious. The guilt-ridden, slow-moving, hand-wringing individual who feels over-

whelmed by guilt and personal inadequacy can be studied. There may be subtler physiological evidences of anxiety; the elevated blood pressures of a minority of men at military induction stations, the hypermotility of the stomach and intestines on X-ray examination of tense persons after ingestion of radiopaque liquid, and the diarrhea of some students before crucial examinations are a few such physiological signs.

Anxiety can be more precisely described by a person who has articulate, or even professional, comprehension of it. Thus, a psychiatrist or a clinical psychologist can note whether he is at ease or apprehensive, confident or self-doubting, and relaxed or muscularly taut in response to things which are going on between himself and a patient during an interview.

Anxiety can be viewed as a warning signal. Physical pain gives warnings in many cases; it informs a person that his ankle is not merely sprained, but probably is broken, and that he should not walk on it until it has been X-rayed and put in a cast. It tells a person that something is wrong with a throbbing tooth and that he should make a long overdue visit to a dentist. Anxiety—that is, emotional pain—acts similarly. It may inform a businessman that he should take a vacation from his ten-hour, six-day week, and it may warn a housewife that she should spend at least two or three half-days each week away from her home and small children. As he notes rising titers of anxiety in himself in various kinds of interactions, a person may become aware of difficulties in his marriage, in his relationships with his children, or in his associations with the people with whom he works.

*Anxiety is always interpersonal in origin.* It always

arises from long-term or short-term unhealthy relationships between people. The ways in which unsound interpersonal relationships can produce anxiety are numerous. An anxious mother who is insecure and apprehensive while caring for her firstborn child, or who finds him disgusting and burdensome because he was unplanned and unwanted, may cause anxiety in the infant, who inarticulately (empathically) perceives the emotional pain in his mother. In a quite different interpersonal context, a marital partner may become anxious as he notes that his sexual approaches cause his partner uneasiness, or even distaste. An elderly salesman may become anxious as he observes that his sales capacities are ebbing and sees impatience in the faces of his superiors. In these very diverse situations, which are simplified for ease of illustration, all the causes of anxiety are *interpersonal*.

Anxiety may occur when an individual, in ways of which he may or may not be aware, feels that his self-esteem and ability to cope with problems are threatened. Severe criticism from someone who is important to him may raise doubts in him about his capacities and worth as a person, and impending failures in his personal, vocational, and social life similarly may assault his feelings of emotional integrity, thus causing anxiety. Interpersonal rebuffs and ruptures of relationships with close people may have the same results. A person who feels that he no longer can cope with his interpersonal environment, or who fears ostracism and exclusion from it, may experience the particularly severe type of anxiety termed panic.

Anxiety may occur in an adolescent who feels unable to adjust to the interpersonal consequences of his

*81*

increasingly strong heterosexual, or homosexual, impulses. It may occur in an elderly individual who notes progressive forgetfulness and feels that incipient senility is robbing him of his ability to be a competent person. It may occur in a middle-aged individual who feels that his personal, physical, and sexual agilities are decreasing and that his hold on his marital partner is weakening. In summary, the feelings of apprehensiveness, dread, depressiveness, loathing, shame, inadequacy, and guilt that may assail people in innumerable kinds of life situations and interpersonal relationships fall under the broad canopy of Sullivan's concept of anxiety.

The interpersonal causes of anxiety are usually both immediate and long-term. This can be illustrated by the following, much-abbreviated example: A thirty-five-year-old man is acutely anxious as he stands before a harshly critical work supervisor who is angry because he bungled a job. In the immediate sense, he is anxious because he fears job demotion, or perhaps loss of his employment. However, from the interpersonal point of view, this anxiety has an extensive history. During the preceding ten years he has lost two other jobs because of similar errors, and he dreads that a third dismissal will confirm both to him and to others his apparent worthlessness as a person. Failure holds a special terror for him, for throughout his childhood and adolescence his domineering father and complaining, guilt-manipulating mother berated him for any shortcomings and gave him little praise for his accomplishments. In addition, throughout his formative years he lacked other close relationships in which he might have obtained a healthier view of himself and

better capacities in dealing with people as a respected equal. The anxiety which this man feels at the moment he is confronting an angry work supervisor thus has a history stretching back through his early adulthood and adolescence into his first childhood experiences. All these contributing experiences are *interpersonal*.

The vulnerability of individuals to anxiety differs much, depending on how healthy or unhealthy their previous life experiences have been. The interpersonal developments of many persons have been relatively sound, and they can endure many kinds of emotional stresses and failures with little anxiety. Other persons have had very damaging interpersonal relationships at various stages in their lives, and relatively minor stresses precipitate much anxiety in them. When anxiety is severe and prolonged, and especially when it causes various kinds of secondary emotional and interpersonal difficulties, the individual having it is said to be psychiatrically ill.

All causes of anxiety have one thing in common. They threaten the individual's feelings of personal worth and competence; they erode his concepts of himself as a capable, esteemed person. Sullivan often uses the word "self-esteem" in his writings and published lectures to indicate an individual's total spectrum of feelings of worth, integrity, and value as a person; he employs "self-esteem" to designate much broader and more basic things than it usually connotes, and an unwary reader of Sullivan's work is likely to be misled by his use of this word. By "self-esteem" he means all the things that hold a person together and make him a human being.

Minor degrees of anxiety are common. Everyone has

small amounts of emotional discomfort (that is, anxiety) each day. In most people these traces of anxiety are minimal and easily tolerated. However, from time to time many persons become aware of larger amounts of anxiety; they warn people that their interpersonal relationships are going askew, or perhaps have long been unhealthy.

When anxiety is marked it has various harmful effects. Strong anxiety impairs, or even paralyzes, a person's capacity to handle his interpersonal relationships. Thus, an individual who is struggling with severe anxiety is much hampered in his ability to cope with marital difficulties, or child-rearing problems, or conflicts with the people with whom he works. This is seen most clearly in the states of intense anxiety termed panic; a panicky person is incapacitated in dealing with other people. A person with a lesser amount of anxiety is, to the extent of his emotional discomfort, imparied in his interpersonal relationships.

These principles may be summarized as follows: *Anxiety (emotional discomfort) is caused by things that are going wrong, or have long gone wrong, in an individual's relationships with other people, and especially the emotionally close people, in his life. However, once anxiety appears it hinders a person's capacities to improve his interpersonal relationships; he is less able to solve the problems that are producing, or have produced, his anxiety.*

Hence, *anxiety has a tendency to bind a person in whatever unhealthy interpersonal patterns he has.* A shy, withdrawn individual tends to be shy and withdrawn in most circumstances; anxiety robs him of the

ability to experiment with new ways of interacting with people and changing his interpersonal patterns. A passive, dependent individual tends to be passive and dependent in most situations; anxiety curbs his capacity to understand what is going on in his life and to alter it.

In many cases a vicious circle is set up. Warped interpersonal patterns cause anxiety, and this anxiety in turn causes the individual to flounder more in his interpersonal life. His emotional adjustment continually deteriorates as mounting anxiety and worsening interpersonal relationships constantly pursue each other.

The major task of psychiatric treatment (discussed in Chapters 6 and 7) is to decrease the various kinds of emotional discomforts grouped under the term "anxiety," and thus to facilitate better interpersonal adjustments.

Anxiety, at least in its more marked forms, has still another harmful effect on a person. It decreases his ability to observe what is occurring in his relationships with other people. A person flooded with anxiety does not perceive clearly the attitudes of the people around him. He does not grasp the implications and consequences of what is happening, or grasps them only partially. In some cases a severely anxious individual goes a step further and begins to misinterpret the attitudes and actions of others. He may, for example, feel that people regard him maliciously, or that they gloat over any distress he has, or, in marked cases, that they deliberately do things to increase his difficulties. Depending on the degree to which anxiety impairs the alertness of his observation of events about

him, and the extent to which it causes him to misinterpret his relationships with people, an individual may be said to be adjusting poorly in an interpersonal situation, or to be psychiatrically ill.

Some persons, in efforts to avoid the pain of severe anxiety, may develop distorted ways of feeling and thinking that are termed neuroses and psychoses. The effects of anxiety on the body may produce psychosomatic disorders such as peptic ulcers and emotionally caused diarrhea. The person who has any of these conditions is, as a rule, *unaware* of the steps by which he is developing a psychiatric disorder in efforts to rid himself of anxiety, or at least to experience it in some less painful manner. The processes by which anxiety produces a neurosis, a personality disorder, or some other psychiatric difficulty lie beyond the individual's field of awareness, and he cannot in most cases become aware of them without some kind of professional help.

## SECURITY AND SECURITY OPERATIONS

Security is the opposite of anxiety. It is a state of relaxed comfort in which an individual feels no apprehensiveness, self-doubt, guilt, inadequacy, or any other kind of emotional distress. Though he usually is not clearly aware of it, each person is at all times seeking to arrange his interpersonal life in ways that give him security.

Complete security—that is, a persistent state of anxiety-free emotional comfort—is a constantly receding goal that no one ever reaches. Each person's life situa-

tions are too complex and changeable, and his interpersonal capacities are too limited, to allow complete emotional comfort for more than brief periods. Every individual all his life is attempting to improve his interpersonal relationships in order to decrease his anxiety and achieve more security. Anxiety and security are on the opposite ends of a seesaw; as one goes up, the other goes down. Security is more than just the absence of anxiety; it is a state of emotional ease, self-confidence, optimism, and comfort in many kinds of interpersonal situations.

In his continual efforts to reduce anxiety (emotional discomfort) and to increase security (emotional comfort) each person uses many types of interpersonal devices which Sullivan calls *security operations. A security operation is a kind of interpersonal action or attitude which, in ways of which he often is unaware, a person seeks to abolish anxiety and to become emotionally at ease.* The concept of security operations is basic in Sullivan's thinking.

A security operation may be healthy or unhealthy. A *healthy* security operation achieves its goal of diminishing anxiety and increasing security without interfering with the individual's interpersonal competence and without causing him any kind of emotional distress. In most instances a healthy security operation increases the smoothness of a person's interpersonal functioning and augments his sense of well-being and adequacy.

An *unhealthy* security operation, on the other hand, reduces anxiety and increases security *at a certain cost to the individual.* The kinds of costs are extremely varied. They may be limitations in the person's interper-

sonal capacities, or they may consist of some kind of emotional discomfort. Thus, an unhealthy security operation may produce a limited degree of emotional suffering, but that suffering is less than the pain of the anxiety which the person would have felt if he had not employed the unhealthy security operation.

From the point of view of emotional well-being, unhealthy security operations are, of course, undesirable and do not work well; they work only sufficiently to blunt a person's anxiety. Moreover, *unhealthy security operations (that is, unhealthy ways of reducing anxiety) produce the wide variety of interpersonal warps, emotional discomforts, and behavioral maladjustments which constitute psychiatric symptoms and psychiatric illnesses.*

In the following paragraphs we shall examine healthy and unhealthy security operations in more detail, and shall give specific examples of them. It is important to remember that each security operation, whether healthy or unhealthy, *is interpersonal in nature*; it occurs in the context of an individual's relationship with another person, or with a group of persons. It is *not* an unobservable process going on in something called the "mind."

*Healthy Security Operations.* Less is known about healthy security operations than about unhealthy ones. In general, healthy security operations function smoothly and go unnoticed. Each person notes them neither in himself nor in others. As a rule they are observed and studied only by mental health professional workers and behavioral scientists.

Unhealthy security operations, on the other hand, produce interpersonal maladjustments and emotional

distresses that in many cases are quickly apparent both to the concerned person and to people around him.

One of the most common, and easily defined, healthy security operations is *sublimation.* In sublimation a person discharges, and gives expression to, uncomfortable feelings in interpersonally acceptable ways. Sublimative security operations often are socially and economically constructive. The nature of sublimative security operations is illustrated in the examples which follow; in each of these examples the emotional and interpersonal processes have been made elementary to ensure clarity.

Security operations are frequently employed to discharge hostile feelings. Each person struggles with at least a certain amount of hostility within himself; no marriage, parent-child relationship, or work situation is completely harmonious and free of hostility. If each person were to express in words or actions all his hostility, most interpersonal relationships would be unworkable.

Each individual therefore has ways of discharging much of his hostility in socially acceptable, and perhaps even constructive, ways. In every work situation, for example, each person must stifle much of his irritability and anger so that the work team can function smoothly. A person in that work situation may, however, get rid of some hostility and feel much satisfaction when the football team he supports defeats the favorite team of one or more of his work associates, and he may gloat over their humiliation. Hostility similarly may be sublimated in aggressive sports, political partisanships, commercial rivalries, and many other competitive activities. In each of these situations people

may be sublimating hostility that arises in other kinds of interpersonal settings—marital relationships, parent-child relationships, sibling relationships, work associations and others.

We can *see, hear,* and *feel* the hostility that arises between people in a work situation, and we can *see, hear,* and *feel* the satisfaction and release of hostility a person has in bantering with his work associates about the defeat which his favorite football team inflicted on the team they back. However, we cannot see, hear, and feel the *connection* between the two. The connection between yesterday's hostility and today's release of it is in many cases not directly observable. It must be conjectured; we must assume it is there. This, from a logical point of view, is a defect in Sullivan's system, but one which is present to a much greater extent in virtually all other psychiatric theories.

In order to observe more directly the discharge, through sublimation, of hostility, a simpler situation must be examined, and in it there should be no time lag between the arousal of hostility and its release. Such an example follows: A woman and a man have an argument, and the woman stomps out of the room, muttering that the man is stupid, and slams the door behind her. Feeling better after that, she finds it easy to make up with the man. In this simple interchange we can *see, hear,* and *feel* directly the connection between the woman's hostility and its sublimation by stomping, name-calling and door-slamming. Such sublimation is, of course, much better than releasing her hostility by slapping the man or throwing hot coffee at him; such nonsublimative hostile acts would make later reconciliation more difficult, or perhaps im-

possible; they would damage, or perhaps destroy, the couple's relationship.

In this incident the woman is reducing the anxiety (emotional distress) she would feel if she did not sublimate her hostility, and afterward she has a higher level of security (emotional comfort).

Another security operation, which often works in a healthy way, is *selective inattention*. In selective inattention an individual (in ways of which he is not aware) fails to observe a stressful or emotionally repulsive thing that is occurring in an interpersonal relationship in which he is involved. He simply blots it out from his perception. Selective inattention is illustrated in the following commonplace example.

A marriage, to be workable, requires a fair amount of selective inattention. A wife does not observe the admiring looks her husband casts at attractive women, nor does she link such looks to her own flat chest or buttocks. Likewise, a husband does not note similar glances his wife gives business friends of his. If everyone observed everything—if each person did not frequently employ the security operation of selective inattention—most interpersonal relations would be intolerable.

Selective inattention is an *interpersonal* process. However, like sublimation, its operation can be clearly observed only in simple situations; it must be conjectured in complex ones. We shall deal at much greater length with selective inattention in Chapter 7, since selective inattention causes special problems in psychotherapy, and is not always healthy.

Another security operation, which may operate in healthy or unhealthy ways, is called by Sullivan the

"as if" process. In an "as if" security operation an individual behaves "as if" he were someone other than himself in an interpersonal situation. He adopts and acts out a role; the role is false, but it nevertheless makes practical and comfortable an otherwise painful interpersonal situation. The "as if" security operation is illustrated in the following example, which is made superficial for clarity of presentation. A fifty-year-old woman in her third marriage finds herself married to a domineering, arrogant, well-to-do man. She cannot come to grips with the fact that he is arrogant and tyrannical, for that would probably lead to the pain of yet another marriage failure; it would also leave her in an economically difficult situation in middle age. Instead, in ways of which she is not clearly aware, she employs an "as if" security operation. She adopts the attitude that her husband is a brilliant, successful man whose judgment and abilities are outstanding, and that it therefore is reasonable to defer to his opinions in almost all matters. She thus avoids coming to grips with his insensitive domination of herself and others; she behaves "as if" he were a great man and she were a dedicated admirer of him. As mentioned above, "as if" security operations are reasonably healthy in some cases, but when they involve marked distortions of reality they become unhealthy.

Sullivan briefly describes other healthy security operations; however, they overlap the three listed above. For example, the things he calls "substitutive processes" are similar to sublimative and "as if" security operations. The field of healthy security operations deserves more exploration than it has so far received.

*Unhealthy Security Operations.* An unhealthy secu-

rity operation reduces anxiety, and increases security, at the cost of producing a personality warp or some type of emotional symptom; if the personality warp or emotional disturbance is severe enough, it constitutes a psychiatric disorder.

The operation of an unhealthy security operation is illustrated in the following example, which, like the others employed in this chapter, is simplified for the sake of clarity and brevity. A fourteen-year-old child has intense hostility toward his parents, and the wish that they were dead briefly flits through his awareness; this thought, and the strong feelings attached to it, arouses much anxiety in him. He deals with his anxiety and guilt by developing, in substitution for the death wishes toward his parents, a persistent dread that he himself will abruptly die of heart disease. Despite repeated reassurances by cardiologists that he has no heart disease and is no more likely to develop it than anyone else of his age, he remains preoccupied with the fear that he either has fatal heart disease or is constantly in imminent danger of developing it. This type of persistent thought, an obsession, is sufficiently long-lasting and painful to justify labeling it a psychiatric symptom. The adolescent's dread is painful to him, but it is less painful than coming to grips with his hatred of, and death wishes toward, his parents. These are the essential characteristics of an unhealthy security operation; a person develops a distressing personality warp or emotional symptom in order to avoid the even greater pain of confronting major interpersonal problems.

Unhealthy security operations cause a large number of the states which are labeled psychiatric illnesses.

However, detailed examination of them, and of the psychiatric disorders they produce, lies beyond the scope of this book, which seeks to provide only a basic introduction to Sullivan's ideas.

## THE SELF-SYSTEM

A problem in discussing the self-system, a basic concept in Sullivan's system of thinking, is his use of various terms for it over the years. Over a span of about two decades he employed the words *self, self-dynamism,* and *self-system* to indicate the same thing, and unfortunately he rarely made this clear. He shifted from one term to another, and sometimes back again, without specifying that they were synonyms. This can be a major stumbling block to the unguided reader of Sullivan's articles and published lectures and seminars. In the last year or two of his life, however, he settled on *self-system,* excluding the other two terms.

The term *self-system* (as well as either of the other two terms) is misleading. Various psychologists, of whom George Herbert Mead is perhaps the best known today, have used the word "self" in ways quite different from the ways Sullivan did. Furthermore, the words "self" and "system," as employed in everyday speech, have meanings much different from that which Sullivan embodied in "self-system." However, the concept of the self-system is so basic in Sullivan's approach to psychiatry, and his use of this expression is so frequent in his writings and lectures, that any attempt to select another term to supplant it would be confusing.

The concept which Sullivan wished to indicate by the word *self-system* is more accurately conveyed by the term *self-protecting system. The self-system is composed of all the security operations by which a person defends himself against anxiety and seeks emotional security. Restated in different words, the self-system is composed of all a person's characteristic, customary interpersonal devices for protecting himself against emotional distress and for seeking more emotional comfort.*

The self-system may be likened to a circle of protecting devices which defend a person from assaults by anxiety. It also may be likened to the circular walls which shield a citadel against attacks, or to a coat of resistant metal which protects an object against corrosion. However, these similes err by suggesting a static situation. The self-system is continually in a state of dynamic movement and change.

The self-system, or self-protecting system, is an abstract concept. It is not observable; it is merely an intellectual convenience that embraces many things, in the same sense that "truth" and "beauty" are intellectual conveniences and not objective things. Sullivan understood this and made it clear in his lectures. However, *the self-system is composed of security operations, and they are not abstract*; security operations are observable interpersonal actions, attitudes, and processes.

When we deal with a person we are constantly in contact with his self-system; he is continually employing security operations to reduce his anxiety and increase his security in response to the continual minor, and at times major, stresses inherent in all interperson-

al relationships. *The total of the security operations that he characteristically and commonly uses in his interpersonal relations constitutes his self-system.* Since the kinds of stresses that each person faces vary from moment to moment, the security operations which he employs are constantly changing.

In every two-person interpersonal relationship one self-system is, in a sense, interacting with another self-system as each participant seeks to protect himself from emotional distress (anxiety) and to achieve emotional comfort (security). In multiple-person interpersonal relationships the interactions are obviously much more intricate.

Sullivan remarks that, when the complexities of these self-system processes are considered, it is remarkable that so many interpersonal relationships work so well most of the time. There are two basic reasons why they do so. Firstly, sound interpersonal relationships are what most people are trying to achieve most of the time; they put a lot of work into this, though usually they are not aware of it. They are mobilizing their security operations (that is, using their self-systems) not only to reduce anxiety and remain comfortable, but also to achieve close, satisfying relationships with others. By selective inattention, sublimation, "as if" operations, and many other security operations they avoid feelings that might otherwise wreck their relationships with people.

The second reason why so many interpersonal relationships function reasonably well despite the conflicting needs and clashing security operations of people, is that personality functioning operates according to a principle which Sullivan terms *the tendency toward health.*

The principle of *the tendency toward health* is best explained by first examining its application to physical health. When the human body's extremely intricate biochemical and biophysical processes are considered, the statistical chances that something serious will go wrong at any moment, impairing the health or destroying the life of a person, are great. There are millions of biochemical and biophysical reactions going on each minute, perhaps each moment, in every person. On a statistical basis it would seem probable, indeed almost inevitable, that some of these processes would break down or develop serious defects constantly. However, they don't. If they did, all humans would be dead or incapacitated within thirty days. To describe this fact it is permissible to say that there is a *basic tendency toward health.*

The same thing is true of interpersonal relationships, and of the complex security operations and self-systems involved in them. On a statistical basis it would seem probable that something would go drastically wrong in each interpersonal relationship every minute, or at least every day. But this does not occur. Most people get along fairly well with most other people much of the time. Thus, Sullivan says, *there is a basic tendency toward emotional health and sound interpersonal functioning. If other things do not interfere, personalities tend to grow in healthy ways and interpersonal relationships tend to proceed in a sound manner.* The problem in a garden, he says, is not the flowers; it is the weeds. If the weeds are eliminated the flowers grow well.

The tendency toward emotional and interpersonal health presumably is a product of man's evolution during millions of years; if this tendency had not devel-

oped man would not today be able to live in complex societies which, if they do not function ideally, at least operate reasonably well.

However, the complexities of interpersonal relationships, security operations, and self-systems also explain why personality warps and emotional problems are common. In various parts of this book we shall indicate some of the ways in which they can go wrong, thus producing psychiatric difficulties, and in Chapters 6 and 7 we shall examine Sullivan's methods of psychotherapy for treating them.

### AWARENESS AND UNAWARENESS

In each of his interpersonal relationships a person is *aware* to some extent of what he is doing and of his reasons for doing it, and he is in some degree *unaware* of these things. For example, a woman may be *aware* that she is bickering with her husband because he badly dented the fender of their car, but she is *unaware* that much of the hostility she is expressing about the fender arises out of more basic conflicts in their strife-ridden marriage.

Awareness and unawareness are fundamental concepts in Sullivan's system of psychiatry, and they differ much from the concepts of "consciousness" and "unconsciousness" of Freud, Jung, and others. Freud, for example, viewed the "unconscious mind" as a definite, biological thing which he felt he had discovered. He felt that many feelings, thoughts, complexes, and urges were locked in this unconscious mind, and could be released and beome conscious only through psychoanalytic treatment.

Sullivan rejects this concept. He feels that the "un-conscious mind" is a metaphorical concept which Freud invented, and that its existence can no more be demonstrated than the existence of other metaphorical concepts such as "the hand of fate" or "the finger of destiny." These things can never be *seen, heard,* or *felt*; they are beyond the possibility of any kind of ob-servation, and belief in them rests on faith or opinion rather than scientific demonstration. As pointed out earlier in this chapter, because of the way such meta-phorical concepts are set up they can never be proved or disproved. Moreover, since the "unconscious mind" is incapable of scientific demonstration, each person is free to speculate in whatever way he wishes about what goes on in it, and this is one of the main causes of the current disarray in psychiatry.

However, a person's *awareness* or *unawareness* of something can be objectively demonstrated by talking with him about it and by observing his actions. It is, moreover, a matter of common observation that every person is *unaware* at each moment of many aspects of what he is doing and his reasons for doing it, and that the ease with which he can become *aware* of these things varies much from one individual to another and from one occasion to the next.

This may be made clear in a simple example. A sur-geon who is performing an appendectomy is, at the time he is performing the operation, aware only of the technical problems involved in his task and the medical reasons why he is performing this operation. However, even on this most superficial level of his awareness he does many things in unaware ways. For example, his fingers fly rapidly through the move-ments of tying surgical knots to shut off bleeding arter-

ies; he does not think through each movement of his fingers as he ties the knots. When he was an intern twenty years previously he spent many hours learning to tie these knots with surgical thread looped over the arm of a wooden chair; at that time he was aware of each movement as he thought it out and directed his fingers in it.

This surgeon is unaware of many other things while he is performing this operation. He becomes irritable with the intern and nurses who are assisting him; when asked why he is irritable he replies that he is not getting from them the kind of alert, skillful assistance they should give. However, his irritability is owing to other things of which, at the time of the operation, he is unaware. Three days previously he examined this patient, felt there was nothing seriously wrong with him, and told him and his family physician that he had only a minor, transient intestinal disorder. When he reexamined the patient four hours before the operation he was chagrined to discover that he in fact had appendicitis; the operation is now more difficult, and more serious for the patient, because the three-day delay has allowed the appendix to become more inflamed, and perhaps gangrenous or adherent to other abdominal organs. It would be emotionally painful to the surgeon to become aware that his irritability during the operation is owing to his anxiety about his misdiagnosis, the resultant increased peril to the patient, and the difficulties he is having in removing a gangrenous appendix. Hence he is aware only that he is irritable, and attributes his irritability to any small clumsiness or lack of alacrity in his assistants. These are all *interpersonal* processes which an informed, astute observer in the operating room could note.

However, the pain of becoming aware of the true reasons for his irritability would be relatively mild, and he therefore could easily become aware of them if someone pointed them out to him. If, for example, the patient's family physician, who had followed the case for the preceding three days and knew all the facts, were present in the operating room to observe the operation, he could say, "Relax, John; the nurses and the intern are doing a good job. You're upset because you missed this diagnosis three days ago and the operation is more difficult and dangerous now. However, this could happen to any surgeon." If the surgeon had a reasonably stable personality structure, he could accept this and recognize its validity. In doing so, the surgeon's *unaware* thoughts and feelings would become *aware,* and a healthier interpersonal situation would be established in the operating room. This is a simple illustration of *unaware* and *aware* thoughts and feelings on the most superficial level of emotional functioning, but it provides a beginning point for examining this complex subject further.

This surgeon is unaware of many other things of a deeper, older nature which contribute to his tenseness and irritability during the operation. He was reared by a cold, critical father and an unaffectionate mother, and he emerged from childhood and adolescence with a constant need to prove to himself and to others that he is an esteemed, useful person, and not an inadequate, worthless one, as his childhood experiences have led him to feel he is. His need to prove his worthwhileness to himself and others formed much of the motivation that led him to become a physician. This same nagging need causes him to be tense, and often irritable, when things go wrong in an operation he is

performing, or in some other aspect of his professional work.

These relationships from his past life obviously are not in the focus of his awareness while he is performing the operation; he is intent on his immediate task. However, depending on a large number of factors, he may or may not be able to become aware of the painful relationships of his formative years when he is not engaged in an attention-absorbing activity. Also, he may or may not be able to become aware of their relationship to the tenseness and irritability he has when things go wrong and his self-confidence is shaken, as in an operation he is performing.

If this surgeon has a high degree of awareness of his personality structure and how it was influenced by the experiences of his early life, he may, in essence, be able to say, "I am aware that the way I was brought up leads me to be very tense, and often irritable, when things go wrong in ways that undermine my self-confidence and self-esteem. My father was constantly critical of me and my mother paid little attention to me. Both of them held my older brother up as a model whom I could never equal. All my life I've been on a treadmill·to prove to myself and others that I am really a capable, worthwhile person. When I make a mistake in diagnosis, or have dificulties during an operation owing to my own misjudgment, I feel anxious and threatened, and I often become impatient with the interns, nurses and others." The clarity with which this surgeon can become aware of these things, and the precision with which he can express them, vary from one day to the next, and perhaps from one hour to another, depending on his changing emotional states,

his interpersonal setting at any moment, and many other factors. That is, his awareness varies much in degree at different times in his life.

On the other hand, a surgeon with this type of background and these kinds of emotional problems may find awareness of the unhealthy relationships of his childhood and adolescence so painful that he cannot easily face the things that went on during his formative years and recognize how they still affect his interpersonal relationships. In this case he might, *in essence,* say, "My father, in his earnestness to help me, tried always to point out to me the ways in which I was wrong. My mother was not the kind of person who showed her feelings much, but she was devoted to me and frequently urged me to follow in my older brother's footsteps." In this case the surgeon camouflages his father's harshness and critical irritability and his mother's coldness and depreciation toward him; by clinging to these false views of what went on in his childhood he can remain unaware of the painfulness of his developing years and of the current personality problems which he developed in them.

The ease with which a person can become aware of the true nature of the interpersonal relationships of his childhood and adolescence, as well as his current relationships with people, varies much from person to person, and from one occasion to another in the same individual. For example, the surgeon described in the preceding paragraph may, while discussing boyhood events with a lifelong friend, abruptly or gradually become aware of the actual nature of some of his childhood and adolescent relationships. In addition, he may then be able to see how these old interpersonal re-

lationships often cause him to be tense and irritable. In many cases, however, insight of this kind can be achieved only in psychotherapy.

Whether or not such insight is necessary, or even advisable, depends on how severe the interpersonal problems of this surgeon are; it also depends on his total life situation and other factors. If his tenseness and his irritability with people are mild and infrequent, there may be no need for such awareness. If, on the other hand, these problems are disturbing his marriage, spoiling his relationships with his children, and damaging his professional practice, psychotherapy is an urgent necessity. Even social and economic factors of a more general sort may influence the need for insight. If, for example, he is the only thoracic or cardiovascular surgeon in his community, he may continue professionally busy and prosperous despite his personality problems. If, on the other hand, he is one of six general surgeons in his community, the insight gained through psychotherapy may offer him his only chance of escaping professional ruin.

*Sullivan views the relationship between awareness and unawareness as very flexible.* Freud's concept of the "unconscious mind" may be likened to a metal box in which feelings, thoughts, urges, and complexes are padlocked, and which can be opened only by the key of psychoanalysis. Sullivan's concept of awareness and uawareness, on the other hand, may be likened to a tide, carrying in it many things; it flows and ebbs to and from a person on the beach.

From Sullivan's point of view, awareness and unawareness are characteristics of specific current or past interpersonal relationships and emotional processes.

In the same sense that a person's feelings about something may be strong or weak, or painful or comfortable, they may be aware or unaware at any particular moment. Detached from specific past or current interpersonal events and emotional processes, awareness and unawareness have no meaning. The concepts of Freud, Jung, and others about the "unconscious mind" are quite different. For example, from Freud's point of view the "unconscious mind" can operate more or less independently of the individual's interpersonal world much of the time; it is a definite biological thing which exists in the central nervous system by an elaborate set of laws of its own.

For Freud, the unconscious mind is a *thing,* and everything that is in it is unconscious by virtue of being there. For Sullivan, unaware thoughts and feelings are those thoughts and feelings which are not in the person's focus of awareness, and which can be brought into it with varying degrees of difficulty; some thoughts and feelings can pass from unawareness to awareness with relative ease, and others can be brought into awareness only with the aid of systematic professional help. The unconscious mind and its elaborate mechanisms can never be observed or studied in the true scientific sense. Since awareness and unawareness are merely qualities of thoughts and feelings, they can be objectively studied by interviewing people, by observing their actions, and by other techniques.

Over a period of almost two decades Sullivan used a confusing variety of terms in talking about awareness and unawareness; these terms include "witting," "unwitting," "overt processes," "covert processes," "dis-

sociation," and others. At times he employed these terms interchangeably and at other times drew subtle, perplexing distinctions between them. An unguided reader of Sullivan's works often becomes lost in this maze of terminology. In this book none of these overlapping terms will be used; only the terms "aware," or "awareness," and "unaware," or "unawareness," will be utilized. At the time of his death Sullivan was in the process of abandoning the earlier expressions and was talking merely of the various degrees of awareness; this obviously was an improvement in the presentation of his ideas.

*A person who is unaware of the nature of his interpersonal experiences learns nothing from them;* he therefore tends to repeat unhealthy patterns of interaction frequently, even though these patterns often cause pain both to him and to others. This is illustrated in the following example. A man with an exasperating job customarily comes home irritable because of problems at work. Because of the irritability he carries home from work, he frequently bickers with his wife and his adolescent son over small things which he would overlook at other times of the day. This happens day after day because the man is *unaware* that he is carrying hostility from his work situation into his family setting. *Unawareness robs him of the ability to profit from experience,* and the same unhealthy interpersonal pattern is repeated innumerable times. Moreover, in time unawareness, and the unhealthy interpersonal events it precipitates, cause new problems; for example, this man's relationships with his son and wife begin to deteriorate.

Sullivan expresses this in a striking way; he says that

*106*

*a person who is unaware of something in his interpersonal life simply does not experience it.* It is as if the event had not occurred; it does not become a part of the experience on which he can draw in his subsequent interpersonal activities. Moreover, if a person's unawareness of things in his interpersonal life is extensive he is likely to have many problems with people, and much emotional distress, because he simply does not have the fund of experience and information he needs to modify his interpersonal patterns and to adapt to the continually changing circumstances of his life. In addition, any personality disorder, or neurotic trait, or other emotional disturbance which the person develops tends to persist since the experiences which would help him improve live outside his range of awareness.

In contrast, when a person *is aware* of the nature of events in his interpersonal relationships he often is able to modify his feelings and actions in healthy ways. Awareness is like the compass which directs a ship back onto its correct course when it strays from it.

Sullivan emphasizes that awareness and unawareness are *ongoing processes.* An individual who is unaware of many things in his interpersonal environment is continually failing to observe, to experience, and to comprehend things that are occurring in his relationships with people.

Sullivan also stresses that awareness and unawareness, though they occur only in the *present,* strongly affect a person's comprehension of his *past* and his views of the *future.* For example, a person who throughout his childhood and adolescence was criticized and depreciated, *today* sees himself as inade-

quate and inept; he consequently views his performance in the *past* as bungling, and feels that he cannot expect educational and vocational success in the *future*. In reality, he may be a talented and capable person, but his unawareness of his abilities clouds his view of his past and cripples his performance in the future. By its nature, awareness can occur only at that pinpoint in time called the present, but by strongly affecting each person's concepts of his past and future it plays a decisive role in molding his life course.

*The cause of unawareness is anxiety.* Abrupt confrontation with the things he excludes from his awareness usually makes a person feel anxiousness, guilt, shame, loathing of himself, or some other form of emotional discomfort. Hence, the ease or difficulty with which a person *can become aware* of things in his interpersonal and emotional life depends on the degree of anxiety he would feel if he did so. When that amount of anxiety is small he may by himself, in the course of his day-to-day experience, be able to develop awareness of various aspects of his life; this enlargement of awareness may be gradual or sudden. The same may occur when anxiety is moderate, but it is less likely. When severe anxiety blocks awareness an individual can in most cases achieve it only with psychotherapeutic help.

As will be discussed at length in Chapters 6 and 7, one of the major tasks in psychotherapy is to decrease the anxiety that is constricting the patient's awareness in many aspects of his life. Increased awareness then allows a person to develop healthier ways of feeling, thinking, and interacting with people. Once this process is set in motion it often acquires a momentum of

its own. As an individual, because of increased aware-ness, includes more things in his field of experience, he is able to come to grips with other anxiety-laden areas of his life and to develop healthier ways of living in ever-wider spectra of interpersonal activities.

# 3

## The Interpersonal Approach to Various Aspects of Emotional Functioning

### PARTICIPANT OBSERVATION

SULLIVAN employs the concept of *participant observation* to define (1) the nature of psychiatry and its allied professions and the data which they study, (2) the basic roles of psychiatrists, clinical psychologists, psychiatric nurses, and other mental health professional workers, and (3) the nature of psychotherapy.

The principle of *participant observation* states that *the basic process in which a psychiatrist, or other mental health worker, is engaged is the informed observation of one or more interpersonal relationships in which he is an active participant.* For example, in psychotherapy a therapist is engaged in an interpersonal relationship in which he is alertly *observing* what is going on between himself and the patient; he is also affecting the nature of that relationship by how he *participates* in it. Similarly, a therapist doing group psychotherapy with six patients is *observing* the interactions of a seven-person interpersonal field in which he is an active *participant.*

*111*

We shall examine in detail the three aspects of *participant observation* listed above.

## THE NATURE OF PSYCHIATRY AND ITS ALLIED PROFESSIONS, AND THE DATA THEY STUDY

Sullivan defines psychiatry as the study of interpersonal relationships, and the use of such relationships to treat interpersonal and emotional disorders. This study and treatment are carried out by professional persons who participate actively in the interpersonal fields they are observing.

Psychiatry is *not* the study and treatment of patients' emotionally caused symptoms and disturbed behavior by aloof, uninvolved persons. A person who is observing a patient *always alters the patient's behavior and emotional reactions by forming the relationship with him that makes observation possible.*

For example, the emotional state and the data a patient gives a psychiatrist during his first interview are much influenced by whether the psychiatrist says at the beginning of it, "Perhaps you could begin by telling me something about whatever problems bring you to see me," or "Lie down on this couch and talk as uninhibitedly as you can," or "First of all, we must establish whether you can pay for this treatment." The psychiatrist's opening words may comfort, or perplex, or anger the patient. The patient's emotional state and behavior in his interviews with the psychiatrist are at once affected by the way the psychiatrist *participates* in the two-person interpersonal field he is *observing.* The concept that a psychiatrist can get from a patient

data which is uninfluenced by the psychiatrist's behavior is, Sullivan states, absurd.

The data which the psychiatrist gets is influenced, moreover, by subtler factors than those indicated in the various opening comments above. It makes much difference whether the psychiatrist speaks in a tone of aloof coldness, or alert professional interest, or irritability. It also is important whether he is at the time searching for a pen on his desk, or glancing at his wristwatch, or looking at he patient. Even the time may affect the patient's responsiveness; at ten in the morning the psychiatrist is more likely to be alertly attentive than at five in the afternoon. The interviewer's gestures, facial expressions, body movements, and all other *nonverbal* features have a strong effect on the patient's emotional state and behavior, and greatly influence the kind of information he gives.

Sullivan stresses that data may be grossly distorted by artificial ways of collecting it. He feels strongly that psychiatric information is valid only if it is collected in the usual kinds of interpersonal relationships in which people live. When exchanging information people usually sit, or stand, in face-to-face situations in which an active interchange of both verbal and nonverbal messages occurs. When a psychiatric interview, or group process, is set up in any other way the therapist in most cases gets misleading or uninterpretable information. This is one of the reasons why Sullivan objects to Freudian, on-the-couch, free-associational psychoanalysis. He feels that the kind of information the therapist gets is much distorted by the unnatural interpersonal relationship set up. The same objections can be made to many of the procedures and interview

techniques employed by behavior therapists and some other kinds of psychotherapists.

Sullivan expresses many of these things succinctly when he says that *the data of psychiatry is always interpersonal.*

### THE ROLE OF THE PSYCHIATRIST OR OTHER MENTAL HEALTH PROFESSIONAL WORKER

A psychiatrist's *role* is to *participate,* as an expert on interpersonal relationships and emotional functioning, in *observing* and helping a person who has problems in these areas; this is also the basic role of any other kind of mental professional worker. He does this by aiding the patient to become aware of many aspects of his life of which he was unaware, and by enabling him to develop new ways of feeling and interacting with people. In this work he uses his relationship with the patient as a therapeutic tool.

Sullivan emphasizes that, in addition to the therapist's effect on the patient's behavior, the patient continuously has an impact on how the therapist is feeling, thinking, and behaving in the interview. The therapist is not, as it were, in a theater observing the patient on a distant stage; he is on the stage with the patient participating in the ongoing relationship between the two of them. A therapist inescapably develops feelings in that relationship, and by being aware of his feelings he learns something about the patient. For example, a therapist notices that the continual, nagging complaints of a patient mobilize a certain amount of irritability in him, and he comprehends the

reactions of the patient's family, who are daily exposed to these complaints; the therapist thus grasps more accurately the emotional atmosphere in which the patient lives.

A further implication of Sullivan's concept of participant observation is that *in psychiatric there is no entirely objective information. Psychiatric information is always to some extent distorted by the process of collecting it.*

This is owing mainly to two factors. Firstly, the patient-therapist relationship is not an ordinary one; it is an artificial relationship because of its investigative and therapeutic qualities, and this artificiality always introduces at least minimal distortions into the data obtained. Secondly, the information the therapist gets is always distorted to a certain degree by his involvement in a relationship with the patient. Any school of psychiatric thought that ignores these distortions as it gathers data and formulates theories runs grave risks of falling into serious errors.

This principle is somewhat similar to the Heisenberg "uncertainty principle" in physics. Heisenberg, the 1932 Nobel laureate in physics, pointed out in 1927 that because of the limitations of human beings as observers there are inevitable boundaries in the knowledge that man can ever achieve in his understanding of the atom and the universe; this is the essential point of Heisenberg's complex principle. Sullivan points out that because of the limitations of human beings as collectors of psychiatric data (owing to their unavoidable status as participant observers in gathering that data), there are always limits in our grasp and understanding of psychiatric information.

The concept of participant observation defines psychotherapy. Psychotherapy is a process in which one person who has expert knowledge in *observing* and understanding interpersonal relationships and emotional functioning *participates* in an interpersonal relationship with another individual who needs help in these areas. The operation of participant observation in psychotherapy is discussed at length in Chapters 6 and 7. The concept of participant observation also defines the role of a therapist doing group psychotherapy, as well as the roles of psychiatric professional staffs working with patients in interpersonal programs on hospital wards.

## PARATAXIC DISTORTIONS

Sullivan adopted the concept of parataxic distortions, and the term, from Thomas V. Moore, who first employed it in his psychiatric writings in 1921. Moore demonstrates the individualism of many psychiatrists in the first three decades of this century. He was ordained a Catholic priest in 1901 and was graduated from the Johns Hopkins Medical School in 1915. He then took his training in psychiatry. He was intermittently active in the Washington, D.C., area, first as a psychologist and then as a psychiatrist, from 1903 to 1924; Sullivan knew him professionally in the last two years of this period. In 1924 Moore abandoned psychiatry to enter the Benedictine order and died in a monastery in northern Spain in 1969 at the age of ninety-one. If it had not been for Sullivan's use of the con-

cept of parataxic distortions, and his meticulousness in noting his debt to Moore for it (Sullivan sometimes referred to Moore using his Benedictine title of Dom Thomas V. Moore), Moore today would be forgotten in psychiatry.

*A parataxic distortion occurs when an individual treats another person as if he were someone else, usually a significant, close person from the individual's past life.*

The nature of a parataxic distortion is made clear in the following example: A twenty-five-year-old man throughout his childhood had a hostile relationship with a loveless, domineering father, and during his adolescence he rebelled strongly against his father and quarreled constantly with him. Now in his adulthood, this man finds himself in frequent conflict with an older male supervisor at work. He resents orders from the supervisor and often argues bitterly with him. The young man's co-workers repeatedly point out to him that the supervisor is a reasonable man, and in time the young man can see that his rebellion against the supervisor is unjustified; however, his irritability and argumentativeness continue. In this situation the younger man is carrying an interpersonal pattern from a previous period in his life into a current one. He is treating the older man as if he were his father, and in doing so he has a parataxic distortion.

In the last couple of years of his life Sullivan broadened the concept of parataxic distortions to include *all kinds of interpersonal events in which a person's feelings and behavior toward another person, or persons, are warped by unhealthy relationships with close people earlier in his life.*

Parataxic distortions occur to a certain extent in most

117

human interactions. Each interpersonal relationship is molded by its participants' past experience, and since there have been minor defects and dissatisfactions in all a person's past relationships, each individual has at least minimal parataxic distortions in each of his interpersonal contacts. In the vast majority of instances these distortions are so small that people overlook them. A parataxic distortion is said to be present, as a rule, only when the problem which a person carries over from a previous relationship causes him significant difficulties in living.

In talking about parataxic distortions, Sullivan says that in every two-person relationship other "imaginary" persons from the past intrude. If the interpersonal field enlarges to include three or more people the interplay of actual persons and parataxic "ghosts" from their pasts becomes complex.

Parataxic distortions may to a certain extent be apparent to many people in day-to-day situations. For example, a marital partner may say to his mate, "When you sulk you're acting just you always did with your father when you couldn't have your way," or, "Every time you spend a couple of days with your mother you come back and argue with me in the same way you argue with her."

In most cases, however, neither the person carrying out a parataxic distortion nor the people around him are aware of it. Thus, the man who had a hostile relationship with his father and who now bickers constantly with his older male supervisor at work sees no connection between these two relationships; he attributes his current quarrels to what he feels are the older man's resistance to new business methods or simply

sees him as an unreasonable, difficult person. Quarreling marital partners rarely see how one or both of them is carrying childhood and adolescent interpersonal warps into the marriage.

Identifying and exploring parataxic distortions constitutes one of the most useful techniques of psychotherapy. The therapist and the patient can investigate two general types of parataxic distortions. Firstly, they can examine parataxic distortions that gradually become evident in the patient's life as he discusses his relationships with his marital partner, his associates at work, his social acquaintances, his children, and others. As it slowly becomes clear that the patient's feelings toward people and his behavior with them are not justified by circumstances, the question arises as to how one or more close relationships from his past are entering into and contaminating his current relationships.

The second type of parataxic distortions that can be examined in psychotherapy is that which occurs in the patient's relationship with the therapist. This relationship is in most cases the only one that is available for the direct scrutiny of the therapist. In intensive psychotherapy the patient begins to feel and behave toward the therapist as if he were some close person from the patient's past. When this happens the therapist points out to the patient the incongruities of his attitudes and behavior. He says, in essence, let us try to discover whom it is from your past that you perceive in me; when we find out, and explore that relationship in detail, we shall probably learn much about what goes on between you and many people in your day-to-day life.

119

A parataxic distortion can give much information to an alert observer. It may do this in a therapeutic situation, a vocational situation, a social setting, or some other context. When an individual's interaction with one or more people is discordant with the realities of his life situation, an observer may ask, "In what ways are one or more close relationships of this individual's past deforming the interpersonal relationships in which he is now involved?" A sure answer cannot be given unless the observer knows a good deal about the life history of the individual, but astute speculations may be made. For example, a person who reacts to every interpersonal frustration with temper-tantrumish tirades in many instances was reared by parents whom he could manipulate by such behavior, and a person who becomes apprehensive and apologetic each time he is criticized was probably reared by people who made him feel guilty and inadequate about each thing he did wrong.

Severe parataxic distortions contribute to many kinds of interpersonal disorders and psychiatric illnesses. In some cases marked parataxic distortions constitute the disorder; for example, a person whose central problem is profound passivity, which enables everyone to dominate and exploit him, may be reacting to each individual in his life as if that individual were a domineering, depreciating parent. In many other kinds of psychiatric disorders parataxic distortions play roles which are important but are less evident on casual inspection; the parataxic distortions often are disguised by the person's psychiatric symptomatology.

In Chapter 4 we shall again consider parataxic dis-

tortions in the context of Sullivan's tripartite division of the development of the infant and young child in the prototaxic, parataxic, and syntaxic phases of experience.

The origin of parataxic distortions lies in defects of consensual validation, which is the subject of the following section of this chapter.

## CONSENSUAL VALIDATION

Sullivan employs the term "consensual validation" to designate the process by which unhealthy interpersonal patterns are corrected. In consensual validation a person arrives at a healthy *consensus* with one or more people about some aspect of his feelings, thoughts, and interpersonal relationships, and this consensus is *validated* by repeated experiences which emphasize its soundness.

A simple kind of consensual validation occurs in learning to talk. A two-year-old child, for example, achieves a consensus with his parents and siblings that the hairy, tail-wagging animal around the house is to be called a "dog." Everyone agrees on this *consensus,* and it is *validated* by many further experiences with dogs. In time the child learns that this vocal sound "dog" is represented in writing by the letters d-o-g, and this general consensus is also validated by repeatedly reading in books, newspapers, and letters about many d-o-gs in various types of situations. The child similarly learns that the particular dog in his house is by general agreement called Fritz, whereas various other dogs have other names.

Consensual validation begins at about twelve months of age and from then on functions continuously. Its operation is illustrated in the following simplified example: A three-year-old child playing in his backyard is accosted by a five-year-old child from the neighboring house; the five-year-old child takes the three-year-old's ball from him and shoves him down when he tries to get it back. Puzzled, fearful, and angry, the three-year-old runs indoors and tells his mother about the incident. She replies that the five-year-old is a bully and telephones the five-year-old's mother to get the ball back; she also complains tactfully that the five-year-old pushed her child down. The ball is returned, and thereafter the five-year-old comes less frequently into the three-year-old's yard.

In this simple event the child and his mother reach a consensus that the five-year-old child is a bully; that consensus is validated as the child watches and hears his mother telephone and get the ball back. The consensus is further validated when the child that evening hears his mother tell his father at the dinner table about the incident, and the father agrees with her opinions and actions and cites two other instances in which he saw the five-year-old act in the same way.

If, on the other hand, consensual validation between the child and his parents in not reached in this situation, the child may have much emotional distress. Also his views of himself and of his relationships with his parents, and with people in general, may be unhealthily affected. If consensual validations are not reached in many situations of this kind, the child may develop a parataxic distortion.

For example, using the same incident described

above, consensual validation is *not* reached in the following sequence of events. When the child comes in and tells his mother how he was pushed down and his ball was taken away, she says, "It probably was your fault. What did you say to annoy him? And why can't you share your things with other children? Why are you so selfish?" In this case no consensus is reached. The child knows that without provocation he was bullied, shoved down, and robbed. He feels puzzled, fearful, and angry, and his mother confuses him and makes him anxious by blaming him and criticizing him. He cannot correlate his feelings with the feelings and actions of his mother. Worse still, he feels a painful interpersonal gap opening between his mother and himself. Instead of consensual validation achieved by healthy communication, he feels anxiety, guilt, and helpless anger. He also feels isolated; he feels that, at least in this instance, his mother has little understanding of his problems, and perhaps no interest in them.

If this is an atypical incident in his childhood its ill effects are erased by later healthier interactions between him and his mother, in which consensual validation is achieved. However, as noted briefly above, if this incident is characteristic of his relationship with his mother throughout his childhood and adolescence there is a marked risk that an unhealthy interpersonal pattern, with much anxiety, will become ingrained in him, and that he will carry it into his later relationships with other people. When he carries this pattern of feeling, thinking, and behaving into later relationships, he has a parataxic distortion created by defective consensual validations earlier in life.

The operation of consensual validation to resolve an

incipient parataxic distortion in a child is shown in the following case vignette. Throughout the first five years of her life a girl, who is an only child, is continually criticized and depreciated by a domineering, loveless mother. By the time she is five this girl, who has led a somewhat isolated life, feels that she is an inept, inadequate person who causes trouble and annoyance to others. She feels vaguely guilty and ill-at-ease much of the time. She carries into other relationships this interpersonal pattern which she has developed with her mother; she is passive, shy, and easily dominated by both children and adults. In ways of which she is unaware, she reacts to everyone as if each person were like her mother, and expects criticism and domination in all her interpersonal contacts; in other words, she has a parataxic distortion which contaminates all her interpersonal relationships.

When she reaches the age of five her father changes jobs; he no longer travels out of town several days a week, but is home each evening. Also, since she is older he begins to take her places with him and to associate more with her. Her father does not criticize, depreciate, and dominate her, but treats her as a worthwhile, likable person. Occasionally he says, "Don't feel bad when your mother bawls you out; she's like that with everyone." Gradually the girl and her father reach a new consensus—that the girl is a valued, attractive person, that she ought not to let other people dominate her, and that her mother has instilled in her an erroneous concept of herself. As in many cases, this new consensus is reached in a slow, piecemeal manner without ever being precisely formulated in words; it is more *felt* than verbalized.

When this girl begins to attend school and to have

more associations in the neighborhood, she has further opportunities to validate her new concept of herself and to test out her interpersonal capacities. She finds that she is treated with respect and friendliness by most children and adults. Her passivity, timidity, and feelings of guiltiness and inadequacy recede still more; she increasingly views herself as a worthwhile person who can live with people as a comfortable equal. *By consensual validation a parataxic distortion in living has been corrected.*

However, regardless of later opportunities for corrective interpersonal experiences, *in some cases the person's anxiety is so strong that it obstructs the operation of consensual validation, and the parataxic distortion persists. In other words, the patient's emotional discomfort in later contacts with people is so marked that he cannot enter into the healthy interpersonal relationships that would help him.* For example, if the girl described above has such severe feelings of anxiousness, guilt, and inadequacy that she cannot participate in the activities which her father offers her, she is blocked from experiences in which consensual validation might occur. If she fears criticism, depreciation, and rebuffs from her father each time he tries to reach her, and withdraws from him, she has no opportunities to get from him valid views of herself and her relationship with her mother.

In a similar manner, if her timidity and sense of inadequacy are so marked that they prevent her from forming close relationships with children and adults at school and in other social situations, no consensual validation occurs in those settings. Anxiety—embracing, in Sullivan's terminology, all kinds of emotional pain—prevents it. She thus emerges into adolescence

and adulthood with an ingrained unhealthy pattern of interaction with people; that is, her parataxic distortion is entrenched.

When consensual validation operates as in the first of the two illustrations above, involving the five-year-old girl, a healthy circular process is set in motion. As the individual becomes increasingly comfortable in his relationships with people he has larger numbers of interpersonal contacts in the various areas of his life. These new relationships offer yet more opportunities for healthy consensual validation, which makes the person still more at ease with people. The process thus acquires an autonomous momentum, moving the individual toward emotional health.

In other cases an unhealthy vicious circle is set in motion. The original interpersonal relationship creates strong anxiety, which in turn blocks the individual from having new, helpful interpersonal contacts. Since he does not become emotionally involved with new people he remains fixed in his small original circle of anxiety, parataxic distortions, and interpersonal isolation.

Sullivan points out the importance of language in consensual validation. He feels that it occurs most effectively after a person has acquired reasonable facility in speech. Thus consensual validation operates mainly from the age of three or four onward. It achieves its full potential after the age of five or six, when skill in language is combined with a marked expansion of interpersonal life at school, in the neighborhood, and in other social settings.

Sullivan feels that, despite the importance of language, much consensual validation is achieved by nonverbal means; that is, it occurs through experience

that is only partially put into words. The individual grasps things in unaware or dimly perceived ways. However, subsequent crystallization in words makes such consensual validation firmer.

The general social environment outside the home of a child or adolescent can aid or inhibit the operation of consensual validation. For example, if the five-year-old girl described above lives in a crime-ridden, brutal slum there is much less chance that consensual validation will help her in her day-to-day associations in her neighborhood, school, and other social environments than if she lives in a comfortable suburb. Similarly, as Sullivan somewhat autobiographically points out, a child reared in an isolated rural setting is less likely to have experiences that lead to healthy consensual validation than a child reared in a situation in which he has many opportunities for constructive experiences. Throughout his writings Sullivan often stresses that extensive social reforms are needed to give each child maximal opportunities for consensual validation in sound social contexts.

All the examples of consensual validation that are given in this chapter occur in unplanned, spontaneous ways in family groups and social situations. As will be discussed in Chapters 6 and 7, consensual validation also can occur in professionally planned ways in psychotherapy. Systematic, deliberate consensual validation is a major technique in Sullivan's system of psychotherapy.

## The Principle of Reciprocal Emotions

Sullivan's principle of reciprocal emotions provides a useful way for looking at interpersonal relationships.

It states that *in every interpersonal relationship*

(1) *the needs of each person are met or not met,*

(2) *the interpersonal patterns between them are integrated in healthy ways, or are disrupted in unhealthy ways,* and

(3) *each person forms expectations for satisfactions or rebuffs of his future needs in this relationship.*

The principle of reciprocal emotions views interpersonal processes in terms of (1) *needs*, (2) *patterns of interaction*, and (3) *expectations for the future*. It also emphasizes that *both* (or *all*) persons in an interpersonal field have needs to be met, interpersonal patterns to be integrated or disrupted, and expectations for the future to be formed.

*Needs* fall into two broad categories—physical and interpersonal. An infant, for example, has physical needs that must be met by others; he must be fed, kept warm, cleaned, and handled with tenderness. The physical needs of older children, adolescents, and adults are subtler because the individual has acquired the ability to satisfy his basic needs without the aid of others. Nevertheless, he has needs for genital sexual activity, reassuring physical contacts with others, and special care when he is sick or otherwise unable to care for himself.

However, once the basic physical needs of infancy have receded into the past, the commonest needs of people are interpersonal. Each person needs relationships which reduce his anxiety and give him emotional security. He needs frequent opportunities for consensual validation to prevent him from developing distorted ways of relating to people. He needs vibrant

interpersonal contacts to maintain his self-esteem, protect him from loneliness, and give his life meaning.

The principle of reciprocal emotions can be made clear by outlining its operation in a simple example. A recently married man comes home after a difficult day at work; his work superior criticized him harshly, and since then he has felt anxious, inadequate, and depressed. As he enters his home he *needs* reassurance, affection, and pleasantness. His wife, at the same time, *needs* attentive affection from her newly married husband.

To meet these *needs,* two patterns of interaction may ensue; one is healthy and the other is unhealthy.

In the healthy pattern of interaction the woman notes her husband's anxiousness and discouragement, and she responds with encouragement, reassurance, and helpful affection. The man, finding his interpersonal needs met, responds with a pattern of grateful affection toward his wife. In this instance the emotional *needs* of both of them are met in a sound *pattern of interaction.*

As a result, the *expectations of the future* of both the man and the woman are healthy. The man feels that in times of emotional distress his wife will sense what he needs and will help him. He feels closer to her; in Sullivan's terminology, he is better "integrated" with her. Similarly, the woman received from the man the affection, closeness, and sharing of experiences that she needs. She too feels better "integrated" with her husband.

In a second, unhealthy pattern of interaction, the man's needs for reassurance and emotional support are not met. When the woman finds him taciturn, anxious,

and depressed, instead of cheerful and enthusiastic, she irritably complains that he has come home in a bad mood, that this is not what she expected in marriage, and she sulks. The *needs* of neither one are met. In their *pattern of interaction* each is disappointed and angry. If such interpersonal events are frequent each of them soon develops *expectations of future* disappointment and disharmony in their marriage. The eventual success or failure of this marriage will depend to a large extent on whether the principle of reciprocal emotions functions well or badly in it.

Sullivan uses parent-child interactions in many of his illustrations of the principle of reciprocal emotions. For example, a nine-month-old infant *needs* much tenderness and gentle physical care from his mother. She, in turn, *needs* gratifying responses from a smiling, nestling infant who reaches clumsily toward her. However, if the mother, because of her personality problems or other factors, is physically tense and vocally irritable toward the child, he may respond with squalling fretfulness or apathetic withdrawal. His frequent crying spells or unresponsiveness seem, the mother feels, to justify her irritability and disappointment about the child. Thus the pattern of interaction between them becomes mutually hostile and distant.

This, in turn, affects the *expectations of the future* of both the mother and the child. The mother views with apprehension and revulsion the relationship she feels she will have with the child in his later years. The infant's *expectations of the future* are inarticulate and dim, but he feels that the world, as he vaguely perceives it, and his mother, whom he faintly is beginning

to discern as a person, will give him more emotional pain than comfort. These feelings, unless corrected in later experiences, will have a significant impact on the infant's developing personality.

Each participant in an interpersonal event usually is unaware of how the principle of reciprocal emotions is operating in it. He does not understand how his *needs,* his *pattern of interaction,* and his *expectations of the future* are affected. When some or all of these things are crystallized in words, however, this awareness much increases the chances that unhealthy functioning of reciprocal emotions will be corrected.

So far, the principle of reciprocal emotions has been considered only in two-person settings. It also operates in more complex ways in groups. For example, in a family the needs, patterns of interaction, and future expectations crisscross from one family segment to another. Parents, both as individuals and as a two-person unit, have needs, patterns of interaction, and expectations of the future in relation to their children, and the children, in turn, have needs, interactional patterns, and future expectations in regard to their parents.

In a similar way the principle of reciprocal emotions can be used to examine social groups. Employers and employees, blacks and whites, antipollution advocates and industrialists, and many other paired groups have their needs, patterns of interaction, and expectations of the future. Harmonious functioning of social groups is more probable if the involved parties have at least limited awareness of their needs, the specific patterns of interaction they are seeking, and their future expectations.

Early in his psychiatric career Sullivan pointed out that the theories of various schools of psychiatric thought are based on metaphors taken largely from Newton's mechanical concepts of the physical universe. For example, psychoanalysis is expressed in terms of forces (sometimes represented by vector arrows) which impinge on diverse structures (such as the id, ego, and superego) with varying strengths. The shock of one force colliding with another, or striking a specific mental structure, produces an emotional conflict or a particular feeling state. For example, a force from the superego striking downward against the ego produces guilt feelings, and incursions from the id into the ego cause anxiety.

Sullivan sometimes speaks of the "hydraulic systems" of Freudian theory. In doing so he is referring to still other Freudian metaphors in which dammed-up forces are periodically released through sluices and overflow channels.

Sullivan feels that this is a poor way to view human emotional and interpersonal functioning. After his first few years in psychiatry he saw the need to develop a concept, or set of concepts, which explained emotional and interpersonal functioning without the use of mechanical metaphors. He therefore evolved his concept of *dynamisms*.

Dynamisms consist of energy transformations. Energy transformations are harder to explain than mechanical concepts since energy is intangible, whereas mechanical objects can be handled and their physical movements can be observed. The average person has

more difficulty understanding energy transformations than he does understanding the movements of weights, pulleys, and counterweights.

However, Sullivan feels that the concept of dynamisms is much sounder since human beings are constantly transforming energy in their interpersonal dealings; though difficult, such energy can in some instances be roughly measured. The concept of dynamisms is also consistent with the overall twentieth-century scientific approach to all aspects of nature. Whereas the nineteenth century viewed the universe in terms of material objects and forces, twentieth-century thinking, from Einstein and Planck onward, has viewed the universe, and all things in it, in terms of the flow and transformation of energy. Sullivan understands clearly this added historical dimension of his concept of dynamisms.

A *dynamism*, Sullivan says, *is a relatively enduring pattern of energy transformations which characterizes the interpersonal relationships and emotional functioning of a person.*

Understanding a specific dynamism requires (1) defining the *source* of its energy and (2) tracing its *course* as it travels through emotional processes and interpersonal relationships.

The *source* of the energy of a dynamism lies in physical processes (*needs*) of the individual. It arises out of his biochemical and biophysical functioning. In its *course* this energy undergoes various transformations as it produces, and travels through, emotional reactions and interpersonal relationships. It finds its resolution in some kind of interpersonal event.

The nature of a dynamism can be made clear by de-

scribing one that occurs in infancy. Sullivan himself most clearly illustrates his concept of dynamisms in examples drawn from the first two years of life.

Biochemical and biophysical processes occurring in a six-month-old infant cause him to feel hungry; these processes include lowering of his blood sugar, contractions of his stomach and upper intestines, and other reactions. These processes constitute the *source* of the dynamism's energy.

The energy produces a state of physical and emotional discomfort in the infant. He becomes physically restless and cries, and this summons his mother. Thus, *the course of the energy's flow causes interpersonal contact between the mother and the infant.* She picks him up, presents a bottle or her breast, and feeds him. As she feeds him she cuddles him and talks affectionately to him; her actions, combined with the milk he is receiving, cause him to respond with relaxed satisfaction. *A dynamism, extending from the biological source of its energy to the expression of that energy in an interpersonal event, has occurred.*

In later childhood, adolescence, and adulthood dynamisms become much more intricate; the person has changed from an inarticulate, helpless infant with only the dimmest notions of himself and his environment into a verbally skillful, sophisticated person who has complex ideas about himself and his life situation. He no longer squalls for food; he goes to the refrigerator for a snack, and perhaps then argues with his mother about what he finds there. Social, cultural, and economic forces have had such marked effects on the individual that application of the concept of dynamisms has become a much more difficult process.

The following brief example illustrates a dynamism in a young adult, tracing the *source* and *course* of its flow of energy. In it Sullivan's term "lust dynamism" will be used to indicate a flow of energy which leads to sexual activity between two persons. A young man feels accumulating sexual tensions within him, which are produced by hormonal biochemical processes; they perhaps bring themselves to his attention through tenseness, or partial erection, of his penis as he sits beside an attractive girl in a university classroom. For the young man, this physical tension is the *source* of the dynamism. Over a period of time he forms a friendship with the girl and has many dates with her, and eventually they engage in genital-to-genital intercourse. This is the *course* of the energy of the dynamism; it finds its final expression in a close interpersonal relationship between the two of them; it is assumed, of course, in this much abbreviated example, that a similar lust dynamism is operating in the girl.

The way in which energy flows in this dynamism is influenced by many social and cultural factors. If, for example, one member of this couple is a devout member of a religious sect that prohibits premarital sexual intercourse, the energy flow will be different. Also, if, because of social factors, the parents of either the boy or the girl object strongly to his friendship with the other person, the dynamism may proceed in another manner.

Remembering our definition of a dynamism as *a relatively enduring pattern of energy transformation which characterizes the interpersonal relationships and emotional functioning of a person*, there obviously are other ways in which the lust dynamism of this young

man could proceed. If marked personality problems prevent him from forming a close relationship with the girl he may find release for the energy of his dynamism in daydreaming sexual activity with her while masturbating. If he has sadistic personality problems he may daydream that he slaps the girl several times and forces her to have intercourse with him, achieving orgasm while fantasizing these scenes. If he has masochistic personality difficulties he may daydream that she strikes him repeatedly, pushes him down, and mounts on his supine body to have intercourse with him.

In each of these instances the man's flow of energy proceeds in a way that is characteristic of him; if this pattern endures over a significant period of time it constitutes a dynamism and forms an essential feature of his emotional and interpersonal functioning.

By the time a person reaches late adolescence his dynamisms have been molded by a great deal of interpersonal experience. Interpersonal damage during his formative years, for example, may cause this young man's sexual energy to be directed toward the boy sitting on his left in the classroom rather than toward the girl sitting on his right. If the young man is a preseminary student of a religious denomination that demands chastity of its clergy, he may, though attracted to the girl, sublimate his sexual energy in socially useful, humanitarian work with large numbers of people.

To a great extent, an individual's dynamisms delineate him as the person we know. They produce the distinctive type of interpersonal relationships which, as discussed in Chapter 2, define what a "personality" is.

As indicated above, a dynamism may be healthy or

unhealthy. A markedly unhealthy dynamism constitutes a psychiatric illness; for example, a dynamism in which a person's sexual energy flows forward, and finds expression in, genital activity with persons of his own sex constitutes a homosexual disorder. In discussing psychiatric problems Sullivan often couples the word "dynamism" with a diagnostic label; for example, he speaks of the obsessional dynamism, the paranoid dynamism, the schizophrenic dynamism, and others. In each case he is indicating that energy flows in a recognizably sick way toward its final expression as a psychiatric disorder.

A Sullivanian dynamism condenses into a single process things that in other psychiatric systems are fragmented. For example, the concept of a dynamism embraces the Freudian concepts (and terms) of "instincts," "libido," "mental mechanisms," "cathexes," and many others. A dynamism emphasizes the unity of emotional and interpersonal functioning and, by contrast, points out the artificiality of fragmenting human psychology into many particles and mechanisms.

## SEXUALITY, LUST, AND INTIMACY

Sullivan feels that sexuality is unimportant in emotional functioning and interpersonal relationships until early adolescence. The main molders of personality before early adolescence are parent-child relationships, other family interactions, neighborhood and school associations, and broad cultural and social forces.

Faced with the problem of discussing sexuality in

*137*

ways that would not be confusing to his Freudian-oriented colleagues and students in Washington, Baltimore, and New York (to whom *sexuality* connoted infantile and childhood, as well as adolescent and adult, sexual functioning) Sullivan during the 1930's adopted in its place the word *lust.* *Lust consists of the complex urges, feelings, and interpersonal actions which have genital sexual activity as their distant or immediate goal; lust begins in early adolescence, or perhaps somewhat before then.* By "genital sexual activity" Sullivan means all actions in which the genitals of one or two persons are involved; it therefore includes masturbation and any kind of genital activity between persons of the same or opposite sexes.

By including the phrase "distant goal" in his definition of lust, Sullivan includes those urges in which genital activity can occur only in the distant future, or perhaps never. Thus, romantic adoration of a person of the opposite sex with whom genital activity can occur only after a long, chaste courtship is lustful, and genitally oriented daydreams about a movie or television star are also lustful. Sullivan obviously is rejecting the Freudian concept of sexuality, which he feels is so broad and vague that it is virtually meaningless; also, though he recognizes that rudimentary genital arousal may occur in infancy and early childhood, he feels that it is not a significant factor in interpersonal relationships and emotional functioning at those times.

*Intimacy* is a central concept in Sullivan's thinking. *Intimacy occurs when the well-being of another person is as important to an individual as his own well-being.* Intimacy, as Sullivan defines it, occurs only between persons who are in more or less the same age bracket; it does not occur in parent-child relationships or in

most sibling relationships. It involves closeness between the two persons, profound respect for each other, sharing of experiences and ideas, and a deep concern by each one for the welfare of the other. Intimacy consists of a friendship so absorbing that it has no equal in any of the two participants' other relationships. *However, intimacy does not necessarily involve sexuality (that is, lust); lust and intimacy are two separate things.*

Intimacy first occurs in the late juvenile period (preadolescence), a developmental phase which lasts a year or two, and which is discussed at length in Chapter 5. It thus appears before the physical sexual maturation of puberty and adolescence begins. During this period intimacy occurs only between persons of the same sex; boys form intimate friendships with boys, and girls form similar relationships with girls. *Any lustful activities in these late juvenile (preadolescent) two-person intimate relationships are contaminants of them;* such contamination is unhealthy and potentially damaging to one or both participants. Sullivan uses the terms "close friend" and "chum" to designate the persons involved in late juvenile (preadolescent) intimacy.

This first, brief type of intimacy ends with the beginning of sexual maturation in early adolescence. At this time the yearnings of a person for intimacy shift to individuals of the opposite sex. From this point onward intimacy and lust are in virtually all healthy cases joined. By late adolescence the individual has achieved interpersonal relationships in which intimacy and lust are expressed together, and this general pattern persists for the rest of the person's life.

Sullivan feels that the experience of intimacy offers

*139*

special opportunities for consensual validation and correction of personality warps. The two persons can share viewpoints, feelings, and experiences with an intensity and a frankness that correct previously acquired emotional distortions, and each one can develop better interpersonal capacities. In his intimate relationships of preadolescence, adolescence, and early adulthood the individual can correct parataxic distortions (unhealthy interpersonal patterns) that are not too severely entrenched. These improved personality qualities can then be carried into the individual's relationships with people in familial, social, vocational, and other areas.

## THE ONE-GENUS POSTULATE

Sullivan summarizes much of his thinking in an axiom which he terms the one-genus postulate: *We are all much more simply human than otherwise.* Although he first stated this postulate in print in 1938, he did not emphasize it until the last few years of his life.

In this simple, almost cryptic statement Sullivan seeks to stress various things. First of all, he emphasizes that the similarities between human beings, regardless of differences in culture, social environment, mental health, and other factors, are much greater than their differences. Thus, the likenesses between a successful industrial executive and a long-term institutionalized schizophrenic are greater than their differences; the emotional functioning, intellectual potentials, and interpersonal capacities of the industrial executive and the schizophrenic are much more alike

than dissimilar. Their contrasting life-styles merely hide their similar human qualities. Their fundamental needs, urges, and feelings are identical; they differ only in the ways in which they are expressing these things. They are unlike not in basic nature, but in the manners in which they are coping with the stresses of living.

By this postulate Sullivan also points out that all the things observed in the persons whom we call psychiatrically ill are present to lesser extents in the persons whom we call emotionally healthy; their differences are in degree, not in nature. For example, there is a continuous spectrum ranging from (1) the occasional social embarrassment of a usually gregarious person through (2) the shyness of a reserved person and (3) the seclusiveness of a schizoid individual to (4) the profound withdrawal of a mute schizophrenic. Despite the different social roles they play, these four persons are more similar than dissimilar; *they are all much more simply human (that is, alike) than otherwise.*

The one-genus postulate also indicates that cultural and ethnic factors produce far fewer differences than likenesses among people. An Australian Bushman, a Bolivian farmer, and a New York accountant are more alike than unlike in their fundamental needs, satisfactions, and discomforts, despite their marked differences in physical appearance if they were to be placed alongside one another in their usual workaday clothes.

The one-genus postulate has various implications for psychiatric treatment. It stresses that the therapeutic task is not to change the basic nature of the patient but to help him modify his ways of feeling, thinking, and relating to people in order to live in a healthier

*141*

manner. Concepts of "health" and "sickness," and "improvement" and "cure," become relative. In individual psychiatric treatment one person is helping another person to improve distortions of feeling, thinking, and interpersonal relationships that are present to at least some degree in all of us. In hospital settings groups of people work with other groups to accomplish the same thing.

The one-genus postulate is at this time a hypothesis; it cannot be proved, at least in its broadest implications. Its validation presents innumerable challenges to future generations of psychiatrists, other mental health professional workers, and behavioral and social scientists.

The one-genus postulate is profoundly humanitarian. In a speculative sense it has much to say about the relationships of social groups, racial groups, nations, and blocks of nations. A few of these applications will be briefly considered in Chapter 8.

# 4

## Sullivan's Views on
## Personality Development:
## Infancy and Childhood

SULLIVAN divided personality development into
the following stages:

1. *Infancy,* which extends from birth until the first
appearance of articulate speech. During this period the
infant gradually carves out from his innumerable sensations and perceptions vague concepts of himself, of
objects in his environment, and of the main person in
his life, his mother. Infancy extends from birth until
about one and a half years of age.

The age numbers given throughout this chapter and
the succeeding chapter are mine, not Sullivan's; they
are given since they make a developmental schedule
easier to follow. Sullivan did not specify particular age
numbers for any of his developmental periods. He divided them according to developmental characteristics
(such as the beginning of articulate speech) or interpersonal needs (such as the need for close association
with other children of the same age).

The ages at which these developmental epochs begin and end vary much from one person to another;
they may differ as much as two or three years in various individuals. Moreover, transitions are never

abrupt; one period gradually merges into the succeeding one during a span that may last from several months to a couple of years or more.

2. *Childhood,* which extends from the first appearance of articulate speech to the emergence of a need for close relationships with other children. During childhood, which extends from about one and a half to four, the main emotional tasks of the child consist of establishing healthy, well-integrated relationships with his parents.

3. *The Juvenile Period,* which begins when the child, at about four, develops a strong need for vibrant relationships with other children. It extends until the age of twelve, when physical sexual maturation begins and lust emerges as an emotional force with which the child must deal.

In this book Sullivan's developmental scheme has been modified to include in the juvenile period the phase which Sullivan termed *preadolescence;* preadolescence is also called the *late juvenile period* in these pages. Sullivan gave preadolescence the status of a separate developmental period. Preadolescence occurs in the last year or two of the juvenile period. During preadolescence the individual forms a particularly intense relationship with another person of the same sex and of about the same age, and in this association he first experiences *intimacy,* a nonsexual relationship which is discussed in the latter part of Chapter 3.

4. *Adolescence,* which begins with physical sexual maturation and lasts until the individual develops the repertory of social, vocational, and economic activities which are considered characteristic of adulthood. It

thus extends from about twelve until some time in the early twenties. Sullivan divides adolescence into *early adolescence* and *late adolescence;* he puts the dividing line at the point where the individual establishes a stable pattern for the expression of his lustful (genital sexual) feelings, which is at about sixteen.

Personality never becomes a fixed thing. It continues to be modified by interpersonal relationships, social circumstances, and other forces for the rest of the individual's life. Nevertheless, in the conventional psychiatric sense the basic processes of personality formation occur during the four stages listed above. We shall now examine each of them in detail; infancy and childhood will be covered in this chapter, and the juvenile period and adolescence will be discussed in the succeeding one.

### INFANCY

From the time of his birth onward an infant is continually flooded with vast numbers of sensations. These sensations include innumerable kinds of lights, sounds, smells, tastes, and physical contacts with things and people, and they also include the countless feelings that arise in his own body.

In the first few months of life the infant cannot distinguish between himself and the things and people around him; everything is one seamless, timeless blur. One of the infant's main tasks is slowly to carve out concepts of himself and the world about him from the masses of undifferentiated sensations that deluge him.

In this process the infant gradually distinguishes

*145*

three types of things—*material objects, people,* and *himself.* This process continues throughout childhood and successive developmental periods; to some extent it goes on for the rest of the individual's life. However, its most crucial phase occurs during infancy at what Sullivan calls "a truly amazing rate."

Sullivan utilizes a confusing set of terms in talking about infancy. He couples the words "good," "bad," and "not" with "nipple," "mother," and "me" to form expressions such as the "good nipple," the "bad nipple," the "good mother," the "bad mother," the "good-me," the "bad-me," and the "not-me." In ordinary usage "good" and "bad" mean far different things from what Sullivan wishes to convey, and the manner in which he uses "not" is little better. Unless a reader is well grounded in Sullivan's works he soon becomes lost in this maze of obscure terminology.

In this book, therefore, other terms which convey Sullivan's meanings more clearly will be substituted. For example, in place of "bad mother" the term "anxiety-producing mother" will be used, and in place of "bad-me" the expression "anxiety-ridden me" will be employed. These terms, and others which will be introduced, indicate clearly what Sullivan meant. However, so that the reader may correlate these two sets of terms easily, especially if he goes on to read Sullivan's original works, Sullivan's terms will often be put in parentheses after the respective expressions used here. Italics also will be employed wherever they can increase clarity. This is admittedly somewhat cumbersome, but it is better than losing the reader altogether in Sullivan's eccentric verbiage. Though Sullivan's ideas have had a profound effect on American psychiatry, his terms are little used, and this is to a large

extent owing to their oddness and awkwardness. Some of the reasons for Sullivan's special problems with terminology have been outlined in the biographical sketch in Chapter 1.

## THE INFANT'S FIRST CONCEPTS OF OBJECTS

The first thing an infant distinguishes gradually out of the vast number of stimuli that flood him in his early months of life is the object which gives him food, the nipple. Hunger is an infant's most acute discomfort and food is his prime need; the satisfaction of hunger is his greatest relief. The sensation of hunger and its satisfaction by food occur several times each day, and the infant slowly perceives that a specific thing, the nipple, gives him his food.

The nipple, therefore, is the first *object* of which the infant becomes aware; the nipple may, of course, be composed of latex, or rubber, or his mother's breast tissues. At first the infant probably has no realization that the nipple is something separate from himself, since he has no conception of himself and his environment as separate things; this distinction is gradually made during the early months of life.

After the infant distinguishes the nipple as something separate from himself it slowly begins to take on characteristics. The characteristics which the nipple acquires, in the infant's perceptions of it, are determined by the tenderness, or anxiousness, or hostility which the mother, or anyone taking her place, feels toward the infant and conveys in her handling of him when the nipple is given him.

Sullivan feels that, depending on the mother's prev-

alent attitudes toward the infant, there are two main ways in which the infant perceives the nipple. They are (1) the *emotionally comfortable nipple* (which Sullivan calls the "good nipple") and (2) the *anxiety-producing nipple* (which Sullivan calls the "bad nipple").

*When, throughout much of this chapter, we talk of the emotionally comfortable nipple (good nipple), the anxiety-producing mother (bad mother), the panic-ridden me (not-me) and other things of this sort we are not talking about specific objects or particular persons. These expressions are merely convenient terms for speaking about a wide spectrum of feelings and thoughts that are in an infant or child. They are literary fictions which are useful in trying to grasp how an infant feels and thinks.*

*For example, when we use the term anxiety-producing nipple (bad nipple) we are indicating a wide spectrum of apprehensive, panicky, self-loathing sensations in an infant. The anxiety-producing nipple (bad nipple), the emotionally comfortable mother (good mother), and the panic-ridden me (not-me) do not exist in the sense that grass and trees exist. They exist only in the minds of psychiatrists and other adults who are using these concepts to talk about infants; the infant has only his apprehensiveness, panic, and self-loathing.*

*This is an important distinction. Understanding it helps to avoid the pit into which so many psychiatric systems have fallen. If a person mistakenly believes that these things (good-me, bad-me, and the others) exist in the sense that trees, grass, and other natural objects exist, he soon begins to manipulate them in elaborate ways and to draw false conclusions. For example, the failure of Freud and his followers to recognize that*

such things as the id, ego, and superego exist only in the minds of psychiatrists who are talking about patients, and not in the minds of patients themselves, has led Freudian psychoanalysis into grave errors and has put it beyond the reach of science. Sullivan understands this, emphasizes it, and enjoins it on his students and readers.

With this preface, we shall proceed to examine the infant's first concepts of *objects,* which are the emotionally comfortable nipple (good nipple) and the anxiety-producing nipple (bad nipple).

*The Emotionally Comfortable Nipple.* When a mother handles her infant with relaxed, affectionate tenderness the infant feels it in each of her activities while caring for him. It is conveyed in her physical contact with him, her vocal sounds, and her general manner before, during, and after feeding him. The infant, of course, feels these things inarticulately and nonverbally, but they nevertheless have a profound influence on him. The effects of maternal attitudes on infants have been studied in numerous psychiatric investigations, and are also observable in the day-to-day life of infants.

When the nipple is, in the vast majority of instances, given to him with relaxed tenderness the infant perceives it as an emotionally comfortable nipple (good nipple). Since this is his first perception of an object, and a particularly intense experience, he will tend to view innumerable later objects in the world about him in a similar way. He will be inclined to view the material world in an anxiety-free, confident manner as he proceeds through infancy and childhood.

*The Anxiety-Producing Nipple.* When a mother's

pervasive mood, in dealing with her infant, is characterized by anxiousness, irritability, revulsion and, in some cases, hostile rejection, the infant inarticulately but acutely perceives her attitudes. The infant, in response, feels anxious and emotionally ill-at-ease. However, having as yet no concept of either his mother or himself, he feels his mother's anxiety, and his own emotional distress, as invested in the mother's nipple. It therefore becomes an anxiety-producing nipple (bad nipple).

The anxiety-producing intensity of the nipple varies, of course, from minor to major, depending on the degree of the mother's anxiousness and other unhealthy feelings toward the child. The infant who perceives the nipple as anxiety-producing and menacing will tend to view the material world about him as similarly anxiety-producing and menacing as he proceeds through childhood and later periods. He will tend to see the physical world as a threatening place in which there is little security and comfort.

The concepts of the emotionally comfortable nipple and the anxiety-producing nipple are presented here in a simple manner for the sake of clarity, and we are employing the language of adults to describe the amorphous, inarticulate feelings of infants. However, there is no other workable way to discuss these things. Moreover, as Sullivan points out, the infant in time views many other *objects* in his environment as emotionally comfortable or anxiety-producing; in general, these are the objects that are important in his physical well-being. They include blankets and clothes to keep him warm, fresh diapers to keep him dry and clean, water and towels to bathe him, and many other things.

In all these activities—being kept warm, being cleaned, and being bathed—the mother's ongoing relaxation, or anxiousness, or hostility invest the objects used with comfortable, or anxious, or threatening qualities. In a sense, therefore, we could speak of comfortable or anxiety-producing clothing, bathing water, and many other objects.

The material world around the infant thus becomes invested with comfortable or threatening qualities, depending on how the infant perceives it in the first, overwhelming interpersonal relationship in his life, that with his mother. However, in describing the infant's first impressions of the material world we concentrate on the nipple since, as a food-giving agent, it has a crucial impact on the infant very early in life.

In most cases, of course, a mother varies a good deal in her handling of her child from one day to the next, and often from one hour to another. At the times when she is affectionate and tender the infant perceives the nipple as an emotionally comfortable nipple, and on the occasions when she is anxious, irritable, and upset he perceives the nipple as anxiety-producing.

Thus, Sullivan says, each infant feels that there are two separate nipples in his life—an emotionally comfortable nipple and an anxiety-producing one. He does not comprehend that they are the same material object, the same nipple. The ways in which he perceives it on different occasions are so diverse, because of the mother's various attitudes on different occasions, that he feels that two separate nipples are being offered him on different occasions.

In terms of his general personality development, the crucial thing is how frequently the infant experiences

the nipple in each of these ways. In other words, which nipple—which perception of the world of material objects—dominates? To make this point clear we shall use the artificial but easily grasped terms of percentages. If 90 percent of an infant's perceptions of the nipple are emotionally comfortable, and 10 percent are anxiety-producing, he will tend to emerge a reasonably well adjusted person in terms of his expectations of the material world. However, he will carry within himself traces of his experiences with the anxiety-producing nipple (and other anxiety-producing objects of his early months). These traces will as a rule affect his behavior only when he is under much emotional stress in his later years.

On the other hand, when a large percentage of the infant's experiences have been with an anxiety-producing nipple (and other anxiety-producing objects) he will in infancy, childhood, adolescence, and beyond tend to view the world of material objects with apprehension and insecurity.

When the infant has been so unfortunate as to have a quite high percentage of severely anxious nipple experiences he will tend to react to stress by decompensating into panicky, disorganized states, and this may happen even when he is subjected to little more than the normal stresses of life; such a person obviously is predisposed to develop psychiatric disorders.

Toward the end of infancy these two perceptions of the nipple—the emotionally comfortable nipple and the anxiety-producing nipple—merge into one concept, a single nipple which has within it the possibilities of appearing either comfortable or anxiety-producing. His predominant view of the nipple, and of material objects in general, will be determined by (1)

the main type of nipple (and other object) experiences he had during infancy and (2) the ways in which subsequent healthy or unhealthy forces mold his personality.

All these things are basically *interpersonal* in nature. The nipple acquires comfortable or anxiety-producing qualities because it was presented to the infant in emotionally comfortable or anxiety-producing *interpersonal* ways. *The view of the material world which the infant carries into childhood and beyond is determined by the emotional atmosphere which prevailed as he was introduced to material objects in the contexts of his close interpersonal relationships.*

## THE INFANT'S FIRST CONCEPTS OF PEOPLE

During the fourth to sixth months of life, and continuing through the rest of infancy and beyond, an infant gradually forms concepts of the first close person in his life, his mother. In the same way in which he earlier formed two separate concepts of the nipple, he slowly develops two concepts of his mother. They are the *emotionally comfortable mother* ("good mother," in Sullivan's terminology) and the *anxiety-producing mother* ("bad mother"). Until about the end of the first year of life the infant perceives these two mothering forces as separate. During the twelfth to eighteenth months of life, or so, he fuses them into a single, composite concept of *mother.* This final, fused concept of mother has within it, in degrees that vary much from one person to another, elements of each of the two earlier concepts.

*The Emotionally Comfortable Mother.* Just as an in-

fant has physical needs for food, warmth, and other things, he has a strong *interpersonal* need for *tenderness.* He needs much relaxed, affectionate care. Sullivan feels that the infant communicates this strong need to the mother, who emphatically perceives it and responds wth the tenderness he requires. This to-and-fro interchange of tenderness is the infant's first interpersonal experience. Sullivan feels it is so important that it merits being titled "the theorem of tenderness."

Many pediatric and psychiatric studies (Sullivan cites a few of the early ones) have demonstrated that infants who receive the tenderness they need are relaxed and eat and sleep well; they thrive physically, as well as emotionally. On the other hand, when an infant's needs for tenderness are not met he in many cases becomes apathetic, listless, fretful, and tense; often he eats and sleeps poorly and may be thin and vulnerable to infectious diseases.

The mother's anxiety-free, relaxed tenderness, or the lack of it, is communicated to the child in the ways in which she physically handles him, talks and coos to him, and in other ways deals with him. Out of the blur of continuous stimuli which impinge on the infant from his environment, the child receiving tenderness gradually perceives a person, whom he comprehends is separate from himself and essential in meeting his needs. He thus forms a concept of the emotionally comfortable mother (good mother).

The individual who in the first year of life develops a firm concept of the emotionally comfortable mother will, in childhood and beyond, tend to view all relationships with people as comfortable and relaxed. Since his first close interpersonal relationship is a satisfactory experience he will tend to approach interper-

sonal relationships in general with confident, pleasant anticipation.

*The Anxiety-Producing Mother.* When a mother has marked feelings of anxiety, irritability, or frank rejection toward an infant, these feelings are emphatically transmitted during her frequent physical acts in caring for him. Out of such interactions the infant gradually forms the concept of the anxiety-producing mother (in Sullivan's terms, the bad mother). The strength of the anxiety-producing mother concept (and it is present to some extent in all persons since all mothers are at least occasionally anxious, irritable, and rejecting) depends on how frequently, and to what degree, the infant is exposed to these unhealthy maternal attitudes.

When an infant's dominant mother concept is that of the anxiety-producing mother he will in childhood and later life-epochs tend to view interpersonal relationships as painful and threatening rather than pleasant and reassuring. The anxiety-laden qualities of his first crucial interpersonal relationship will tend to taint his expectations of all later ones.

If the anxiety-producing mother concept is very strong, and the individual consequently has profound discomfort about closeness with people in his later life, he will be more prone to develop psychiatric difficulties than the average person.

*The Fusion of the Two Mother Concepts.* During the latter months of infancy, which is here arbitrarily defined as terminating at the age of eighteen months, the infant fuses the concept of the emotionally comfortable mother (good mother) and the anxiety-producing mother (bad mother) into a single, composite concept of *mother.*

Any particular child's composite concept of his

*mother* will depend on how strong the two contributing mother concepts are. For example (again using the quite artificial but easily understood terms of percentages), if a particular infant's experiences with his mother fall in the category of the emotionally comfortable mother in 90 percent of his contracts with her, and in the category of the anxiety-producing mother in 10 percent of his interactions with her, he will have a predominantly healthy, comfortable composite concept of her. He will tend to enter all later interpersonal relationships with pleasant anticipation.

If, on the other hand, 40 or 50 percent of the infant-mother interactions are contaminated by maternal anxiety, hostility, and rejection, the anxiety-producing mother concept will dominate, and in childhood and beyond the individual will tend to view all interpersonal bonds with apprehensiveness, and perhaps dread.

In our discussions of mother-infant relationships we have assumed that the child's natural mother is caring for him; however, the same kinds of interactions occur, and the same types of concepts are formed, when someone other than the natural mother rears the child; the same processes also occur when several mother figures participate in caring for the child.

During late infancy and throughout childhood the child has increasingly closer relationships with his father and siblings, and he begins to form concepts of them. These concepts are much influenced by the previous patterns of feeling and thinking that were formed in the mother-child relationship. Just as we may speak of the child's impressions of his mother as the emotionally comfortable (good) mother and the

anxiety-producing (bad) mother, we may speak of his concepts of his father as the emotionally comfortable (good) father and the anxiety-producing (bad) father, and of his fusion of these two concepts into the single one of *father* at the end of infancy or during early childhood. In a less intense way, siblings who are close to him in infancy and early childhood, and any other close persons, are incorporated into his views of the world of people. Out of these various interpersonal relationships the child's general views of the comfort or anxiousness of living with people are evolved.

### THE INFANT'S FIRST CONCEPTS OF HIMSELF

In addition to concepts of his material environment and his interpersonal world, the infant also gradually develops concepts of himself. Slowly he becomes aware that he is a distant thing, separate from his material environment, his mother, and all other people.

During the latter half of infancy he evolves three concepts of himself: (1) the *emotionally comfortable me* (in Sullivan's terms, the "good-me"), (2) the *anxiety-ridden me* ("bad-me"), and (3) the *panic-ridden me* ("not-me").

*The Emotionally Comfortable Me.* The concept that a person has of himself during late infancy, or childhood, or any other period of his life is mainly a summation of the kinds of feelings and attitudes that the emotionally close people have demonstrated toward him throughout all his previous years. For example, an infant who in most of his contacts with his mother and others is treated with anxiety-free tenderness and re-

spect will tend to see himself as a worthwhile, esteemed person. In contrast, an infant who is treated with hostility, anxiousness, and rejection will tend to view himself as worthless and inadequate.

Until he is well into childhood a person has no information about what kind of person he is other than that conveyed in the ways close people treat him. During middle and late childhood he slowly gets other data from interpersonal relationships at school, in the neighborhood, and in broader social groups, but these later impressions about himself are superimposed on the earlier, stronger concepts obtained in his more intense relationships.

Anxiety-free, tender care implies much respect for the infant, and conveys to him that he is a worthwhile, loved, and valued person. Out of these feelings he forms the concept of the emotionally comfortable me (good-me). In later childhood and beyond, the person in whom the concept of the emotionally comfortable me is dominant sees himself as an emotionally adequate individual who can engage easily and successfully in close relationships with people and in broader social activities.

*The Anxiety-Ridden Me.* When an infant is cared for in a predominantly anxious, hostile, and rejecting manner he perceives himself as inadequate, worthless, and troublesome; that is, he develops an anxiety-ridden me (bad-me) concept of himself. As indicated in Chapter 2, Sullivan employs the word "anxiety" to embrace the entire spectrum of painful emotions and feelings; it thus includes anxiousness, guilt, shame, feelings of inferiority, and loathing of oneself and others. The anxiety-ridden me (bad-me) includes all, or most

of these feelings, and the individual sees himself as anxious, worthless, shameful, unloved, and unlovable.

*The Panic-Ridden Me.* An infant who is treated with extreme anxiety, hostility, and rejection feels that he is markedly repulsive, worthless, and inadequate. Out of such feelings he evolves the concept of the panic-ridden me (not-me). The panic-ridden me is imbued with eerie,uncanny, chaotic qualities that cannot easily be put into words. The panic-ridden me is perceived and observed only in states of disorganized panic, nightmares, eerie dreams, schizophrenic phenomena, and other kinds of psychiatric distresses later in life. It encapsulates the most extreme kinds of emotional suffering, intellectual bewilderment, and personality disorganization.

From the age of five or six onward, a person can put into words some aspects of the emotionally comfortable (good) me; he can state, in essence: I am a reasonably able, worthwhile person and my relationships with people are good. He also can express some features of his anxiety-ridden (bad) me concept; he can, in essence, say: I am not as worthwhile and adequate as others, and my defects spoil my relationships with other people; I am upset by anxious, hostile, guilty, and shameful feelings. However, an individual *never* becomes able to put his panic-ridden (not-me) feelings into words; the panic-ridden me is always clouded by eerie feelings, anguish, and the sensation of imminent personal disintegration.

*The Infant's Fusion of His Three Concepts of Himself.* The feelings and attitudes of each mother vary much toward her infant from one occasion to another; she often is tender and relaxed, sometimes is anxious

159

and irritable, and occasionally is hostile and rejecting. Each infant hence develops three concepts of himself—the emotionally comfortable (good) me, the anxiety-ridden (bad) me, and the panic-ridden (not) me. However, in late infancy and early childhood he fuses all three concepts into a single view of himself. The nature of this final concept is determined by how strong each of its three component concepts is.

When the majority of the infant's experiences with his mother, and with other mothering persons, have contributed to forming the emotionally comfortable me, he will tend to view himself as a worthwhile, able person who can relate to other people in sound, comfortable ways. However, when a large percentage, or a majority, of an infant's experiences with mothering persons have been in the category of the anxiety-ridden me, he will tend to see himself as an inadequate, depreciated person who is anxious, troublesome, and inept in his relationships with people. If a large percentage of the infant-mother contacts have been in the category of the panic-ridden me, he will tend to be a disturbed person who has major problems in living with people and who deteriorates into agitation and panic when he is under stress; he will be vulnerable to various kinds of psychiatric illnesses in later life unless the damage of infancy is corrected by later, healthier interpersonal experiences.

This process of fusion is well advanced by the end of infancy (eighteen months), but it continues until the age of three or so. After that the three concepts a person has of himself are merged into a comprehensive whole which has characteristics of each of its compo-

nent parts. The dominant concept will prevail most of the time, but adverse circumstances and interpersonal stresses may cause one of the lesser concepts to come to the fore occasionally. Thus, an individual who most of the time operates on the level of the emotionally comfortable me may shift to feeling and behaving on the level of the anxiety-ridden me when he is assailed by emotionally disturbing events. Under extreme interpersonal stress the panic-ridden me may surface.

Thus, the three concepts of *me* exist in varying degrees in all persons from childhood onward. The process of keeping them fused continues throughout life, since interpersonal stresses will tend to detach the anxiety-ridden me or the panic-ridden me and bring it to the surface; when this happens the individual is flooded with anxiety or panic. The relationship of the three me's never becomes static, but a stable equilibrium, with the emotionally comfortable me predominant, occurs in most people. Because of the principle of *the tendency toward health* (Chapter 2), this equilibrium has an inherent tendency to keep the individual as near as possible to the level of the emotionally comfortable me most of the time.

Nevertheless, ongoing interpersonal events and relationships continually influence the equilibrium between the emotionally comfortable (good) me, the anxiety-ridden (bad) me, and the panic-ridden (not) me. Emotionally healthy relationships strengthen the role of the emotionally comfortable me and decrease the strength of the other two me's. Emotionally traumatic events and relationships tend to accentuate the roles of the anxiety-ridden me and the panic-ridden me. How-

ever, the innate tendency of personality functioning is to maintain the equilibrium on the level of the emotionally comfortable me.

## CHILDHOOD

In Sullivan's scheme of personality development, childhood begins when articulate speech first appears and extends until the child develops strong interpersonal needs for association with nonfamily children of his own age group. Sullivan does not specify exact age limits for childhood, but for purposes of clarity we may place it at between one and a half years and four years of age. Sullivan thus uses the word "childhood" in a quite restricted sense; he employs the terms "juvenile period" and "preadolescence" to cover the period from four to twelve years of age.

### THE IMPACTS OF VARIOUS KINDS OF FAMILY INTERACTIONS

Sullivan gives much more attention to the mother-child relationship than to the father-child relationship and sibling relationships in his discussions of personality development. He recognizes the importance of fathers and siblings in the personality evolution of a child, but does not deal with them in detail. He views the mother-child relationship as the prototype of all early, close relationships and examines it minutely; father-child and sibling relationships follow patterns basically similar to those of the mother in their impacts

on the infant and the child. For example, as noted above, we can speak of the emotionally comfortable (good) father and the anxiety-producing (bad) father, and any sibling who plays a large role in a child's life during his early months and years is similarly important. *The course of a personality evolution is molded by all the close interpersonal relationships that impinge on it.* The importance of the father-child relationship and the sibling relationships vary depending on how large a role the father plays in child-rearing and on the number of siblings and the intensities of their relationships with the child.

Thus, in the same way that a child's early relationship with his mother may induce in him feelings of ease or discomfort about interpersonal relationships, a child's relationship with his father may lead him to feel that interactions with people are attractive or threatening. An anxiety-free, affectionate, esteem-building relationship with his father tends to produce in the child capacities for comfortable, healthy interpersonal living, and an anxiety-laden, hostile, cold relationship with his father tends to damage the child's interpersonal capabilities and to give him a distorted view of himself.

The influences of the mother and the father on the child may be similar and reinforce each other, or they may be different and work in opposite ways. For example, a sound father-child relationship and a sound mother-child relationship work together to produce a sound personality. On the other hand, a stressful father-child relationship may undermine interpersonal capacities developed in a healthy mother-child relationship. In some cases a constructive father-child

interaction aids the child to develop personality strengths he did not evolve during an unsatisfactory or even damaging relationship with his mother.

The complex interactions of family members with one another, and the impacts of various kinds of family structures on children's personality development, have been extensively investigated in the decades since Sullivan's death in 1949. There has, on the whole, been a shift away from interest in one-to-one relationships (mother-child, father-child, and others) to multiple-person relationships (mother-plus-father to child, family to child, and others). These studies, with their emphases on the total interpersonal environment of the developing child, strongly reflect Sullivan's influence. Since Sullivan stresses the importance of general social and group influences on personality development, he undoubtedly would welcome this shift as a logical extension of his viewpoints.

Sullivan feels that later interpersonal relationships are more likely to erase earlier damage than to erode personality strength. For example, a child who had a sound relationship with his mother will tend to withstand the stress of a harsh, loveless relationship with his father; he has, so to speak, firm ground on which to stand to resist assaults on his emotional stability. On the other hand, a child who had a damaging relationship with his mother will tend to improve a great deal if he subsequently has a prolonged, close, healthy relationship with his father. In keeping with his principle of *the tendency toward health,* Sullivan feels that constructive, healthy influences dominate over unhealthy ones unless the imbalance is marked. He feels that this principle can be observed in the life histories of patients and in psychotherapy with them.

Throughout this section the term "thinking" will be employed in a broad way. It will embrace all aspects of an individual's perception and evaluation of his experiences.

During his second to fourth years of life a child slowly develops the capacity for *syntaxic* thinking; this is Sullivan's term for realistic, logical thinking, as compared with the more primitive, nonlogical forms of thinking and experiencing that occur during infancy.

Syntaxic thinking enables a child to form realistic appraisals of the people and things around him, or at least to begin to do so. Sullivan also stresses that a certain amount of articulate speech is necessary for syntaxic (logical) thinking. However, syntaxic thinking obviously incorporates nonverbal and poorly formulated thoughts and feelings as well.

To understand Sullivan's concept of syntaxic thinking, it is necessary to outline his three-part scheme of the evolution of thinking, as it occurs in each individual. He divides the development of thinking into *prototaxic, parataxic,* and *syntaxic* phases.

*Prototaxic Thinking.* The earliest mode of thinking, which occurs during the first year of life and then recedes in the following year or two, is *prototaxic.* As discussed earlier in this chapter, an infant at first has no awareness of himself, his material environment, and other people. His experience consists of an unending flood of brief, vague sensations which form a seamless blur. He spends his first twelve to eighteen months slowly carving out of this mass of indistinct stimuli which bombard him a concept of himself as

separate from his environment, and concepts of the material objects and people around him.

For example, a three-month-old infant feels a vague physical distress which in later years he will call hunger. He cries and flexes his arms and legs. He then feels a nipple between his lips. His physical discomfort subsides and he feels drowsy. The infant does not link these four states with each other. He perceives them as separate events which have no connection with each other; in early infancy experience occurs without relationship to time, place, and sequence. The prototaxic mode of thinking may be likened to the confused perception of scenes of photographic slides which are projected in a random, helter-skelter way on a screen, with no continuity or relatedness of subject matter.

The term "prototaxic" is constructed from the Greek words meaning *first arrangement.* In searching for a more easily grasped synonym for *prototaxic phase,* I have elsewhere employed the term *phase of crude sensations.*

*Parataxic Thinking.* In *parataxic thinking* the child forms links between the various fragments of his experience, but these links are haphazard and nonrational; they do not follow rules of logic and cause-and-effect relatedness. The parataxic phase of thinking is dominant during the second year of life, after which it slowly recedes.

In parataxic thought the child links together events that happen close to each other in time, but which are not in fact logically related. The infant also links together events which are similar in some small, striking detail but are dissimilar in their major features.

The word "parataxic" is formed from the Greek words indicating *an arrangement in which things are placed alongside, but unconnected, with each other.* In efforts to avoid the obscurity of the term *parataxic phase* I have sometimes employed the expression *phase of misconnected experiences* as a synonym.

These three modes of thinking (prototaxic, parataxic, and syntaxic) overlap much during the child's formative years, but each one tends to be dominant at a certain period. Also, an individual carries extensive remnants of the two primitive modes of thought, prototaxic and parataxic, into later childhood, adolescence, and adulthood. However, they tend to manifest themselves only when the individual is under much stress, or is very fatigued, or is psychiatrically ill, or is asleep; they are the main molders of dreams.

Sullivan employs the term "parataxic" somewhat differently in his early and late years. In his final mature years he uses it in the very broad sense that has been discussed at length in Chapter 3. Parataxic thought will be considered in this present chapter more along the lines Sullivan follows in his early years, since the child's progress through prototaxic and parataxic thought into mature syntaxic thinking is being traced.

The nature of parataxic thinking in infancy and early childhood is illustrated in the following example, simplified for purposes of clarity and ease of presentation. A fifteen-month-old infant is accustomed to affectionate, prompt care by his mother when he is hungry, wet, or cold. Beginning at about fifteen months of age he notices that late each afternoon, as it becomes dark, his mother disappears for an hour or more. If he be-

167

comes hungry, wet, or cold at this time she comes only if he cries long and loudly. In time he notices that another person, whom he will later know as his father, comes home at this hour. Connecting these two events in a parataxic way, the child feels that his father is maliciously coming between his mother and him; he concludes that his father is hostile to him and is robbing him of his mother's attention. He feels both hostility and fear in regard to his father. The fact is that in the late afternoon his father returns from work, and he and the mother sink into chairs in the family room to have cocktails and exchange news about the day's events. Sullivan feels that during the second and third years of life a child forms a large number of such parataxic distortions as he struggles to understand his environment and his place in it. These parataxic distortions are especially numerous and severe when the child's interpersonal relationships are unhealthy and are contaminated by anxiety, and the more marked a parataxic distortion is, the more entrenched it will tend to be.

In healthy emotional development the vast majority of these parataxic distortions are corrected during the subsequent syntaxic phase of experience and thinking, which begins during the third and fourth years and lasts throughout the rest of life.

*Syntaxic Thinking.* In syntaxic thinking a child develops the capacity for logical, realistic thinking and sound appraisals of himself, other people, and his relationships with them; he also becomes able to think about material objects in logical ways. The word "syntaxic" is derived from two Greek words signifying *an arrangement in which things are linked in harmonious ways.* In an attempt to get away from the obscurity of the term "parataxic phase" I have elsewhere used as a

substitute for it the expression *phase of realistic appraisals.*

The basic process of syntaxic thinking is *consensual validation,* which has been discussed in Chapter 3. In consensual validation a person arrives at a healthy *consensus* (or agreement) with one or more people about some aspect of his feelings and thoughts, and this consensus is validated by repeated interpersonal experiences which emphasize its soundness. In Chapter 3 the ways are outlined in which anxiety can obstruct consensual validation and thus lead to unhealthy patterns of interaction. Since these unhealthy patterns in many cases consist of distortions that occurred originally in the parataxic phase, they are termed parataxic distortions. Parataxic distortions which are not corrected (because of anxiety and various kinds of emotional difficulties) during the syntaxic phase persist into later childhood, adolescence, and adulthood.

Consensual validation gradually becomes dominant during the third and fourth years of life; it continues as the main tool of syntaxic thinking for the rest of life. Sullivan employs the concepts of consensual validation and syntaxic thinking in a closely linked manner; they overlap each other much, and to some extent are synonyms. In a stricter technical sense, consensual validation is the tool syntaxic thinking uses to achieve logical, realistic appraisals.

The operation of syntaxic thinking can be illustrated in the later course of the infant described in the case vignette at the end of the preceding section on parataxic thinking. This infant notes that each day when his father comes home his mother spends less time with him, and he parataxically feels that his father maliciously competes with him for his mother's attention.

If this child during his third through fifth years of life has much affectionate, healthy interaction with his father, he gradually comprehends that his father is neither competitive nor hostile toward him and that his mother's affection for him is not really diminished by the parents' relationship with each other. The child's feelings of hostility and fearfulness toward the father are slowly replaced by feelings of affection and confidence. Through *consensual validation* (mainly in his relationship with his father) this child has resolved a *parataxic distortion* (his prior fear and hostility toward his father, whom he saw as competitive and malicious) and has achieved *syntaxic thinking* in his relationship with both his parents.

If, on the other hand, this father is unaffectionate or harshly irritable toward this child much of the time, or spends so little time with him that the child has no opportunities to evaluate their relationship, the child's fearfulness and hostility toward the father will tend to persist and become ingrained. In later childhood, adolescence, and adulthood he tends to react toward most male authoritative figures at school and at work with hostility and fearfulness; he thus has a severe *parataxic distortion,* since he is treating current figures in his life as if they were a close person in his past life with whom he had a traumatic relationship. *Consensual validation* has not occurred, and *syntaxic thinking* in this area of his life has not been achieved.

Consensual validation and syntaxic thinking occur only in the contexts of healthy interpersonal relationships. When a child's interpersonal relationships are defective, or are marred by anxiety or other con-

taminating feelings, consensual validation and syntaxic thinking cannot occur, and parataxic distortions persist.

Sullivan feels that language plays an important role
in consensual validation and syntaxic thinking.
Although he recognizes the large role of nonverbal
communication (gestures, facial expressions, body
movements, and others) in syntaxic thinking, he nevertheless stresses that consensual validation is largely
dependent on language. He feels that language is crucial in helping a person to crystallize to himself and
others the nature of his feelings and thoughts; the development of language greatly increases a child's capacity to resolve his interpersonal problems and mis-
conceptions. Hence, syntaxic thinking to a large extent
begins with, and accompanies, the development of
language.

Sullivan also feels that language is important in the
fusion of the infantile concepts discussed earlier in
this chapter. For example, clear use of the word
*mother,* or its equivalents, both in solitary thinking
and in interpersonal relationships, aids the child much
in fusing his primitive concepts of the emotionally
comfortable (good) mother and the anxiety-producing
(bad) mother into a mature, single concept of *mother.*
Similarly, language aids the child to fuse the emotionally comfortable (good) me, the anxiety-ridden (bad) me,
and the panic-ridden (not) me into a single concept
of *myself.* Language enables the child to encapsulate
diverse concepts and experiences into simpler ones.
He then can think and talk easily about himself, other
people, and his interpersonal relationships with them.

During childhood (from eighteen months to four years of age) an individual acquires the skills which enable him to move into broader social settings. He becomes more mobile, he becomes trained for control of urine and feces, and he acquires speech. He learns to eat with others at a table, he learns to handle many kinds of objects without damaging them, and he acquires many other abilities which are necessary for sound interpersonal living. *All these things are learned in interpersonal relationships.*

Sullivan emphasizes that a child learns more in the first several years of life than he will during the rest of his lifespan. The child will never again accomplish anything so difficult as the acquisition of language, which requires the mastery of intricate neuromuscular coordinations and an immense body of symbols. The child also learns a complex system of nonverbal communication by gestures, facial expressions, body stances, nonverbal vocal sounds, and other means. He acquires innumerable skills in his eye movements, hand movements, and body movements. All these things, learned in the contexts of interpersonal relationships, enable him to enlarge his sphere of interpersonal activities and to participate smoothly in them.

While he recognizes that learning is a complex process to which a wide variety of things contribute, Sullivan emphasizes that interpersonal rewards and deprivations occupy central roles in all kinds of learning. *The child to a large extent learns in order to gain interpersonal satisfactions and to avoid interpersonal pain.* The child continually strives to achieve close, gratify-

ing relationships with people and to avoid rejection and isolation.

A child learns to eat at the table and to play well with other children in order to gain the approval of his parents and the companionship of other people at the dining table and in the playroom. Failure to learn these things brings disapproval and social exclusion; the child who slops food over others while eating is sent to the kitchen at mealtimes, and the child who cannot play smoothly with other children is soon rejected by them.

Successful learning brings affection and gratifying relationships with others, whereas failure to learn brings disapproval and isolation. In later years the interpersonal forces in learning are subtler but equally important. Throughout life learning retains its essentially interpersonal nature.

Sullivan often employs the word *ostracism* to designate the exclusion of a child from close associations with other children. Such ostracism is mainly the result of the child's failure to learn the interpersonal skills necessary for inclusion in childhood groups, but it, in turn, further increases the child's problems by depriving him of the social relationships in which he would develop better interpersonal skills. Sullivan feels that *loneliness* (he uses this word almost in a technical sense) is so painful that the threat of it constantly goads a child to develop the interpersonal capacities that enable him to escape it.

*Other Developments During Childhood.* The development of a person's *self-system* and *security operations* (Chapter 2) commences during childhood. By the middle of the fourth year they have acquired some of

the features that will characterize the person. In a similar way, all the other personality processes described in Chapters 2 and 3, with the exceptions of intimacy and lust, begin during childhood. By the end of childhood the first outlines of the personality features and interpersonal patterns that will in later years distinguish the individual can be discerned.

# 5

*Sullivan's Views on Personality Development: The Juvenile Period and Adolescence*

## JUVENILE PERIOD

THE juvenile period begins at about the age of four when the child develops a strong need for interpersonal relationships with nonfamily children of his own age group, and it ends at about the age of twelve when sexual maturation ushers in adolescence.

In the personality developmental scheme used in this book the juvenile era includes a period which Sullivan treated separately; Sullivan broke off the last year or two of the juvenile period and called it *preadolescence.* For reasons which will be specified later, this one- or two-year period is here included as a subdivision of the juvenile period.

### THE JUVENILE SOCIAL GROUP AS A
### THERAPEUTIC FORCE

Most psychiatric schools of thought tend to stress the significance of infancy and early childhood, and view later childhood as a quiescent time in which little

175

personality development occurs. Freudian psycho-analysis, for example, holds that when the Oedipus complex is resolved at about the age of six the child enters into a relatively unimportant phase termed the latency period.

Sullivan, on the other hand, teaches that the juvenile period is an important phase of development. He feels that during it the child has many opportunities in nonfamily interpersonal settings to resolve personality problems and unhealthy modes of emotional functioning. In relationships with nonfamily children and adults he can correct any parataxic distortions he acquired in infancy and early childhood in his parental home. In the broader social environments outside his home he can develop healtheir ways of viewing himself and others, and he can evolve new ways of interacting with people.

Until he enters the juvenile period at about the age of four the child's interpersonal world has consisted mainly of the two to five people in his parental home. During the early part of the juvenile period the child's field of interpersonal relationships expands quickly to embrace twenty to fifty, or more, people in his school setting, neighborhood environment, and other social situations. Sullivan feels that in the American social system the school community is the most important nonfamily interpersonal environment of a person during the juvenile period. A seven-year-old child spends almost half his weekday waking hours at school. When schooltime is added to the hours he spends playing with children at school and in the neighborhood, the majority of his time is found to be passed in activities with nonfamily children and adults.

In these settings a child has extensive opportunities

to correct personality malformations. For example, a child who throughout his early years was rejected by a self-centered, emotionally immature mother and criticized and depreciated by a domineering, irritable father, and who as a result feels that he is an inadequate, worthless person, may develop quite different views of himself as he interacts with nonfamily children and adults during his juvenile years. Other children treat him as a worthwhile, capable individual, and teachers and other nonfamily adults give him friendliness and prestige. In these relationships the child may gradually correct the personality warps he developed in his parental home.

The extent to which juvenile interpersonal relationships can help an individual resolve his personality difficulties depends, among other things, on how severe those difficulties are and the extent to which continuing unhealthy home interactions make them worse. A child with mild or moderate home-produced personality problems tends to benefit much from the healthier interpersonal relationships he has in his juvenile years. On the other hand, a child who emerges from infancy and childhood with severe personality difficulties, and who as a result has profound anxiety which cripples him in his attempts to interact in juvenile social groups, is much less likely to improve.

In the latter case a vicious circle sometimes occurs. The child who has marked personality problems because of unhealthy home relationships may be unable to form close associations with people outside his home. He remains anxiety-ridden and socially isolated in his school and neighborhood environments. Thus he has close interpersonal relationships only at home; since he remains mired in the unhealthy home situa-

177

tion that produced his difficulties, his personality problems become more ingrained. Moreover, the juvenile years in which much emotional development might have occurred pass without benefit. Anxiety and interpersonal ineptness bar him from the contacts in which he might improve, and fix him in relationships which accentuate his difficulties.

Juvenile social groups operate in therapeutic ways because they offer more chances for *consensual validation* than the parental home. The child's opportunities for coming to healthy *consensuses* with others about himself and his attitudes, and for *validation* of these consensuses repeatedly in various interpersonal settings, are much greater in school, neighborhood, and other social situations than in his home environment; in broader social settings he interacts with up to forty or fifty people at various times, whereas he interacts with two to five persons at home. The people in large social groups come from many home backgrounds, most of which are reasonably healthy, and the associations the child has with these people give him a wide spectrum of healthy interactions in which he can correct the distortions that were produced in two or three unhealthy relationships in his home.

Moreover, Sullivan feels, a general *social consensual validation* occurs in juvenile groups. The group as a whole develops new ways of looking at themselves and at interpersonal life. The group members develop new ways of interacting, new sets of values, and new viewpoints about themselves that are not characteristic of any single home from which they come. A fresh social consensus occurs which is the common experience of the whole group.

Sullivan feels that all aspects of a child's self-system and security operations can be altered in healthy ways during the juvenile period, and that many of the causes of anxiety in the child's personality can be removed.

Sullivan points out that during the juvenile period a child's emotional health can be damaged if his school, neighborhood, and other social environments are blighted by poverty, economic injustice, intellectual stagnation, widespread vice, and ethnic prejudices. Any or all of these social contaminants can rob children of their possibilities of personality improvement during a crucial phase of their development. This aspect of Sullivan's teachings is particularly in harmony with the broad trends of psychiatric thinking today, and it also distinguishes his viewpoints from those of almost all his contemporaries during the first half of the twentieth century, who put exclusive stress on home interactions and attributed little importance to relationships outside the home.

Sullivan's viewpoints therefore have social implications. Reform of unhealthy social environments is a mental health necessity as well as a humanitarian one. Since the community has a potential therapeutic function in every individual's life it must be maintained in a state of soundness and vitality to fulfill this function.

This subject will be further examined in Chapter 8.


PREADOLESCENCE (LATE JUVENILE PERIOD)

Many commentators on Sullivan, including myself, feel that his concept of preadolescence (in this book called the late juvenile period) represents an intrusion

of Sullivan's own personality problems into his views on psychiatry and personality development. Sullivan's concept of preadolescence, and its rejection by most of his followers, is in this respect similar to Freud's theory of the death instinct (Thanatos), which is rejected by almost all Freudians. Most interpreters of Freud feel that the death instinct theory was the product of his well-known preoccupation with death during much of his adult life, and the accentuation of it in his old age, when he proposed this concept.

Sullivan's concept of preadolescence will be described, and the objections to it will then be considered.

Sullivan felt that during the one- to two-year period prior to the beginning of sexual maturation a separate phase of personality development occurs, and he called it preadolescence. Although this phase can begin as early as eight and a half, it usually occupies only the year or two before the first sexual changes indicate the beginning of adolescence. During this period the individual forms a particularly close relationship with another person of his same sex and age group; Sullivan used the term "chum" to designate this other person.

The bond which each person has with his chum, Sullivan said, is the most intense he has yet had in his life. In this relationship the person for the first time achieves *intimacy,* which Sullivan defined as a two-person state in which each individual feels that the well-being of the other individual is equal in importance to his own well-being. In healthy instances this relationship is not marred by genital sexual activity between the chums.

Sullivan felt that in this relationship each chum has

special opportunities for correcting his personality warps and parataxic distortions, and for expanding his interpersonal capacities. The unique closeness of this relationship also offers each chum many chances for accurate consensual validation and consequent personality growth.

The chum relationship spontaneously dissolves when sexual maturation ushers in adolescence. However, the capacity for achieving intimacy with another person and becoming deeply absorbed in his wellbeing, which each chum developed during preadolescence, *is carried over into similar relationships with persons of the opposite sex in adolescence and adulthood.*

Three main objections can be leveled against Sullivan's concept of preadolescence. First of all, there is little clinical evidence for it; many child development studies indicate that it occurs in very few persons, and that the few persons who pass through this kind of experience tend to develop into homosexuals in later life. Secondly, when Sullivan's personal history in late childhood, adolescence, and beyond is known it becomes clear that he generalized his own emotional maldevelopment into a universal law of personality formation. The details of Sullivan's early years and his own disastrous chumship are given in the biographical sketch of him in Chapter 1. Sullivan's early life experiences were not known to any of his professional contemporaries; they were discovered only when biographical investigations were made many years after his death.

Thirdly, in the last lectures in which Sullivan touched on this subject, he placed much less emphasis

the features that will characterize the person. In a similar way, all the other personality processes described on preadolescence. He seemed to be abandoning the concepts of preadolescence and chumship, and to be shifting intimacy forward a few years into adolescence. This, of course, would make Sullivan's developmental schedule consistent with generally accepted psychiatric viewpoints and would remove the only aspect of his scheme of personality evolution which most professional persons find clearly unacceptable.

## ADOLESCENCE

Adolescence begins with physical sexual maturation and extends, in Sullivan's scheme of personality development, until the individual develops the wide repertory of social, vocational, and economic activities which are considered characteristic of adulthood. It thus stretches from about twelve to some time in the early twenties.

Sullivan further subdivides adolescence into *early adolescence* and *late adolescence*. He puts the dividing line between these two phases at the point where the individual establishes a stable pattern for expression of lustful (genital sexual) feelings, which is sixteen or so.

### EARLY ADOLESCENCE: SULLIVAN'S
### VIEWS ON SEXUALITY

Early adolescence commences at about the age of twelve, when physical sexual maturation begins, and

lasts until about sixteen, when the individual develops a stable pattern for the expression of his genital sexual feelings.

*Sullivan's Views on Sexuality.* Sullivan feels that sexuality first becomes a significant force in emotional functioning and personality development at the beginning of adolescence. As pointed out in Chapter 3, by sexuality Sullivan means more or less what the term signifies in general usage—the impulses, feelings, and thoughts which have as their possible goal some kind of passionate genital activity. In this respect Sullivan differs sharply from Freudian psychoanalysis and other systems of thought which postulate sexual feelings in infancy and childhood and attribute much importance to them. In order to avoid misunderstanding of what he is discussing when he talks about this subject, Sullivan in general avoids the words "sexual" and "sexuality," at least as technical terms; they would have been misleading in the predominantly Freudian circles in which Sullivan worked and taught in Washington, Baltimore, and New York. Instead, he adopts the word "lust," and defines it as *the felt aspects of genital sexual urges.* In this way he emphasizes his rejection of the view that sexual impulses during infancy and childhood play significant roles in personality development. Although rudimentary sexual feelings and phenomena may occur in infants and children, Sullivan feels they are of little importance in personality development.

During adolescence lust impels a person to seek *intimacy* with individuals of the opposite sex; however, the early adolescent spends three or four years developing interpersonal skills and comfort with persons of the opposite sex before he achieves such intimacy. As

pointed out previously, Sullivan defines intimacy as a state in which the well-being of another person is as important to an individual as his own well-being.

Sullivan views lust as the last of the major dynamisms which motivate and direct human emotional processes and personality development. As outlined in Chapter 3, Sullivan defines a dynamism as a relatively enduring pattern of energy transformation which characterizes the emotional functioning of a person; the energy arises from the individual's biological processes and finds its expression in his interpersonal activities. When the lust dynamism and the drive to achieve intimacy are combined during adolescence they form a very strong force in molding a person's interpersonal functioning and emotional reactions.

Sullivan feels that in a two-person heterosexual relationship in which each person finds comfortable expression for his lust dynamism and his need for intimacy there are valuable opportunities for correcting personality warps. In his intense interaction in such a relationship over a period of time, each participant can remedy personality defects formed during his infancy, childhood, and juvenile period; in this relationship he also can develop better capacities for forming healthy, comfortable associations with people in general. Thus adolescence in most cases is a spontaneously therapeutic period of personality growth. Moreover, the forces which cause such growth—lust and the need for intimacy—are present for almost all the rest of adult life.

Sullivan's view of adolescence thus differs appreciably from that of many other psychiatric schools, which look upon adolescence mainly as a period in which a

person's previous personality development is tested by the stresses of his burgeoning sexual impulses and his drives for independence; these other psychiatric schools usually regard any personality growth during adolescence as minor. Sullivan recognizes the turbulence, and often the anguish, of adolescence. He deals extensively with the stresses on personality structure that occur at this time. However, he also feels that in successful, intimate, lustful relationships adolescents have important opportunities for emotional and interpersonal growth, and that individuals who do not grow in this way during adolescence may be ill-equipped for the adjustments of adulthood.

When he speaks of lustful relationships Sullivan does not mean that genital-to-genital contact has to occur (it may be merely a *possible*, remote occurrence); the lesser nongenital forms of lustful affection are adequate if they are accompanied by passionate feelings.

*Lust as an Integrating Force.* Sullivan stresses the central roles of various kinds of integrating forces in personality development. He uses the words *integrate* and *integration* to designate personality needs and emotional forces which draw two or more people together in interpersonal closeness.

Lust is the last of a series of seven integrating forces in interpersonal life; in listing them below, a brief review of personality development from infancy to adulthood will be outlined.

(1) An infant's need for contact with other persons to meet his biological requirements for living—food, warmth, cleanliness, and others—is the first major integrating force; it draws the infant and his mother together in his first interpersonal relationship.

*185*

(2) The next integrating force is the infant's need for tenderness, which evokes tenderness in the mother, or whoever is taking her place. This mutual feeling of tenderness is a persistent force throughout infancy and much of childhood.

(3) The child next has a need for collaborative interaction with guiding adults as he slowly learns to walk, speak, feed himself, master toilet training, and acquire the innumerable techniques required for social living.

(4) Thereafter the child develops a strong need for vibrant relationships with nonfamily children of his own general age group during the juvenile period. In this context he rapidly acquires new interpersonal skills and by consensual validation may correct any personality warps he may have.

(5) He simultaneously has a marked need for acceptance by other children and by nonfamily adults as an esteemed, adequate person in the broader social groups into which he moves.

(6) In the late juvenile period (preadolescence) the person, according to Sullivan's original developmental scheme, develops a drive to achieve a particularly close relationship with a special friend of the same age and sex. In this nonsexual relationship he first experiences the feeling of interpersonal intimacy.

(7) With adolescence comes the final integrating tendency, lust, which draws an individual into close relationships with persons of the opposite sex, in which genital sexual activity is an implied possible goal. His needs for intimacy and his lustful drives are united and directed toward persons of the opposite sex.

Failure to achieve adequate, comfortable expression

and satisfaction of any of these seven *integrating* forces leaves a person to some extent maladjusted in his repertory of interpersonal capacities and modes of emotional experience.

However, such defects can to a large extent be remedied in succeeding periods if later integrating forces operate with sufficient vigor to bind the person in strong interpersonal relationships in which he has ample opportunities for consensual validation, correction of parataxic distortions, and personality growth. The final integrating tendency, lust, has particular importance. Since it is the last of the integrating forces the individual experiences it can combine with previous ones such as intimacy and tenderness. It also continues to operate throughout almost all the rest of the person's life span.

## LATE ADOLESCENCE

Late adolescence begins when a person establishes a stable pattern for the expression of his lustful feelings, and it ends when he achieves the kinds of social, vocational, and economic adjustments which are considered characteristic of adulthood. During late adolescence an individual refines his interpersonal skills as he adjusts to continually changing social, educational, vocational, and economic circumstances.

During the first two decades of life, Sullivan says, a very skillful animal gradually becomes a human being, and the instruments used in accomplishing this task are interpersonal relationships.

Unlike most psychiatric authorities, Sullivan

stresses the role of chance in personality formation. When he speaks of chance he is referring to the kinds of interpersonal environments into which a person is thrown and the unpredictable events, over which he has no control, that occur in them. He emphasizes that a person who is reared in socially unhealthy, culturally barren, economically deprived settings has much less probability of achieving emotional stability than an individual who is reared in more favorable settings. Many sociopsychiatric studies since his time have proved the soundness of this viewpoint.

Sullivan also points out the roles of chance meetings and events in molding personality development. As he speaks of the influence of such things, one feels that perhaps he is looking back over the course of his own life. Certainly his life history aptly illustrates the role of chance in personality evolution. If Sullivan's father had not moved from Norwich, New York, to an isolated, meager farm when Sullivan was three years old, he would have been reared in a more vibrant, varied interpersonal setting and his characterological development would probably have been far different. If Sullivan, a lonely boy hungry for some kind of human warmth, had not at the age of eight and a half by chance fallen into a close, long-term relationship with an aggressively homosexual adolescent boy who lived on an adjacent farm, his sexual history would probably have been healthier, with extensive consequences for the course of his life. If Sullivan had not failed all his courses in his freshman year at Cornell and had not been therefore suspended, he probably would have become a physicist and not a physician. If at the age of thirty he had not been transferred, without initiative on his part, by the government bureau for which he

was working to an administrative post in one of America's foremost psychiatric hospitals, it is doubtful that he would have taken up a psychiatric career.

In emphasizing the role of chance in personality development, Sullivan differs much from other psychiatrists of the first half of the twentieth century. Other psychiatric leaders of his time in general feel that once the basic structure of a personality is laid down during infancy and childhood the life course of a person, from a psychiatric point of view, is fairly predictable; his personality structure determines the relationships he forms, the opportunities he carves for himself, and the social and economic environments he seeks to live in. Sullivan denies this; he feels that blind chance, operating through the vagaries of social and economic events over which the individual has no control, are of marked importance in determining the individual's interpersonal life and psychiatric health or illness. On the whole, Sullivan is nearer the general currents of thought that are tending to prevail in American society in the second half of this century.

If conditions are at least minimally favorable, Sullivan believes, a person can continue to grow emotionally throughout adult life. Personality never becomes fixed and rigid. It can always be modified. Psychiatric therapy is possible only because of this lifelong capacity for change.

## THE INTERPERSONAL APPROACH TO PSYCHIATRIC DISORDERS

It is beyond the scope of an introductory book on Sullivan's work, directed to a broad group of readers,

to give accounts of his views on each of the various kinds of psychiatric disorders. Such coverage would require much space and many illustrative cases, and thorough understanding of it requires an extensive knowledge of clinical psychiatry. The selected, descriptive bibliography at the end of this book lists the works in which Sullivan deals with this subject. A few general comments on this aspect of Sullivan's work will, however, be given.

Sullivan defines a psychiatric disorder as any state in which an individual has inadequate or inappropriate performance in his interpersonal relationships. This definition embraces a broad spectrum of human difficulties, extending from marital adjustments and child-rearing difficulties on one hand to severe personality disorders and psychoses on the other. In addition to its flexibility, this definition implies that the states which are termed psychiatric disorders are to some extent influenced by changing social and cultural concepts about the kinds of behavior that are "adequate" and "appropriate." This definition emphasizes that a person with a psychiatric disorder must always be evaluated in the context of his general interpersonal and social situation.

This definition also implies that a psychiatric disorder can be examined only in an *interpersonal* situation. For example, obsessive thinking, or auditory hallucinations, or severe anxiousness can be evaluated, and thus defined, only after the person who has such a difficulty informs another individual about it. This act of communication, by verbal and nonverbal means, at once sets up a two-person interpersonal relationship which becomes part of the patient's experience. More-

over, the experience of informing someone about his difficulty, and observing the other individual's reactions to it, has at least a small effect on his emotional state. Sullivan stresses that a patient is never in a vacuum. He is always participating in interpersonal relationships with other people; in these interpersonal relationships all involved persons are continually observing one another, communicating by verbal and nonverbal means with one another, and affecting one another's emotional functioning. Sullivan feels that a psychiatric illness makes sense only in the context of the *participant observer* who is interacting with the patient.

This definition also implies that the causes, as well as the manifestations, of a psychiatric disorder are interpersonal. A psychiatric disorder arises out of sick interpersonal relationships, reveals itself in disturbed interpersonal functioning, and is treated by therapeutic interpersonal relationships.

*Sullivan's Coverage of Psychiatric Syndromes.* Although Sullivan developed a comprehensive scheme of personality development and emotional functioning, he did not systematically cover the entire range of psychiatric illnesses. He restricted his teaching and writing to those psychiatric disorders with which he had extensive, direct experience in the care of patients. These conditions were, in the main, schizophrenic disorders, paranoid disturbances, obsessive compulsive disorders, hysterical illnesses, and hypochondriacal conditions; he also discussed various kinds of personality disorders, such as passive personality disorders, schizoid personality disorders, sexual deviations, and others.

He had throughout his psychiatric career relatively little experience in studying and treating patients with depressions, manic disorders, some of the less-common neurotic syndromes, psychosomatic illnesses, and organic brain syndromes. He worked much with adolescents, but little with children. In his lectures and writings he clearly pointed out the fields in which he had had little patient-care experience and, other than occasionally offering brief speculations, did not deal with them.

Such scrupulousness and frankness are unusual in psychiatric pioneers. In their eagerness to round out complete systems of psychiatric thought, most psychiatric innovators write extensively about psychiatric conditions with which they have had little experience; in most cases the writer speculates on the basis of his general theoretical position, or extends principles derived from work with patients with other kinds of disorders. Sullivan felt that this was pretentious and unscientific, and he refused to do it.

Although this books does not systematically cover Sullivan's views on psychiatric disorders, much material relevant to them is found in Chapters 2 and 3 on interpersonal relationships and emotional functioning, Chapters 4 and 5 on personality development, and Chapters 6 and 7 on psychotherapy. For example, the sections on anxiety, the self-system, parataxic distortions, the infant's concepts of the panic-ridden (not) me, and many other sections by their very natures deal with the causes of psychiatric disturbances. Moreover, many of the case vignettes scattered throughout this book contrast healthy and unhealthy interpersonal and emotional processes.

# 6

## Sullivan's Methods of Psychotherapy: Basic Aspects

SULLIVAN developed a system of psychotherapy which has had a profound effect on American psychiatry, and its influence is spreading gradually beyond this country. It is commonly called *interpersonal psychotherapy*. Its diffusion has been the result of Sullivan's influence as a teacher, lecturer, and writer during his lifetime, and the popularity of his book *The Psychiatric Interview* (1954), the best written and most widely read of his posthumously published works.

Many aspects of Sullivan's system of psychotherapy have been incorporated into other psychotherapeutic approaches, including many of the modified Freudian-psychoanalytic techniques. It is the most carefully worked out non-Freudian system of psychotherapy, both in theory and technique; many other psychotherapeutic innovators have taken over parts of it, often renaming them in the process. Much of the spread of Sullivan's methods has occurred in innumerable direct teacher-student relationships during the last forty years, and the extent of his influence becomes apparent only when his techniques are evaluated in the con-

text of what is daily said and done in the vast bulk of American psychotherapy.

## THE PHYSICAL SETTING OF THE
## PSYCHOTHERAPEUTIC SESSION

Sullivan views psychotherapy as an *interpersonal* process in which one person, designated an expert in interpersonal relationships and emotional functioning, helps another person to resolve his problems in living. Hence, the physical setting of the interview should facilitate patient-therapist communication and interaction, and anything that impairs such communication and interaction should be avoided.

During an interview the patient and the therapist sit opposite each other in comfortable chairs separated by the usual space which divides two persons in an earnest dialogue. It is unimportant whether or not a desk separates the patient and the therapist so long as the desk is neither so high nor so cluttered that it obstructs their clear view of each other. The patient should be able to see at any time what impression, or lack of it, his words and actions are making on the therapist, and the therapist should be able to see the patient similarly.

However, Sullivan recognizes that in many cases a patient, especially a shy, apprehensive one, becomes anxious if the therapist looks at him steadily, and that many therapists become uneasy during prolonged eye-to-eye scrutiny by patients. He therefore recommends that the therapist sit in full view of the patient but with his body and gaze turned at a 45- or 90-degree angle

away from the patient; the therapist may sit with his body and gaze directed at a point about three or four feet to the right or the left of the patient. This position relieves both the therapist and the patient of the tension of looking continuously at each other, but nevertheless at any time allows either one to face the other by a slight movement of his head. The therapist can effortlessly look at the patient when making a point, or when he wishes to note the patient's reaction to anything, and the patient similarly can observe the therapist.

The physical arrangement and decoration of the office, including the drapes, lighting, wall ornaments, and similar items, are unimportant so long as they are not distracting. The decorations also should not draw attention to the therapist's personal life. For example, a framed photograph of a former teacher of the therapist hanging above his desk is acceptable, since it implies nothing more than that he has had the customary training of a person in his kind of work. However, a photograph of the therapist's wife and children is unacceptable, since it may distract the patient from viewing the therapist merely as a professional person.

Sullivan himself always learned the patient's full, or customary, name and greeted him with it at the beginning of the first interview. He then briefly reviewed with the patient whatever he knew about him (such as any data the patient's referring physician had given him when the appointment was made); he felt that it put the patient at ease to know at once the extent of the therapist's information about him.

However, the therapist should not confront the patient with information that will frighten him or stifle

his spontaneity; for example, if the therapist has been told that the patient is felt to be suicidal he as a rule does not reveal this to the patient. In those cases, the vast majority, in which the therapist can tell the patient everything he knows of him the therapist may afterward indicate that this is the extent of his knowledge. Sullivan emphasizes the necessity of meticulous honesty with patients; if the patient ever detects the therapist in a deception, "the ball game is over." Sullivan recommends that, by his bearing and words, the therapist should attempt to put the patient at ease; he views this as necessary for the smooth flow of the interview. The therapist should avoid all pretentiousness and pomp that might give the impression that the therapist is a distinguished or important person; such things betray the vanity or insecurity of the therapist and dampen the patient's spontaneity.

With frightened or otherwise upset patients Sullivan sometimes went to extensive, even melodramatic, lengths to put them at ease. One of Sullivan's patients relates that when he came, fearful and apprehensive, for his first interview Sullivan, after briefly excusing himself, spent the first several minutes of the session rummaging through papers on his desk and ransacking drawers in an apparent search for a missing paper, muttering, "Where did I put that thing? Where on earth is it?" By the time Sullivan had located the presumably missing paper the patient had lost his anxiousness and his awe of Sullivan, and could begin the interview in a relaxed manner. Sullivan at times was somewhat histrionic in therapy when he wanted to emphasize a point or clear some obstacle that was hindering the progress of the interview.

Sullivan in his own practice was more flexible than most psychiatrists about the lengths of interviews. Although he usually adhered to the conventional fifty-minute time limit he occasionally extended sessions to an hour and a half or two hours, especially in initial interviews when he was attempting to evaluate a patient thoroughly. The duration of his treatment was likewise quite varied. A series of interviews sometimes totaled ten or fifteen when a limited object was the goal; however, treatment often lasted from several months to two or three years when extensive personality changes were sought.

### The Basic Therapeutic Process— Participant Observation

The basic role of a therapist, Sullivan says, is that of a *participant observer* (this concept is considered from a different point of view in Chapter 3). The therapist is an alert, specially trained *observer* who *participates* in a particular kind of interpersonal relationship with the patient. The therapist uses this relationship and his own personality resources as tools to aid the patient to resolve the emotional problems for which he is seeking help. The interview proceeds actively in a verbal interchange in which the therapist makes comments, asks questions, and operates in flexible ways to help the patient explore his problems. Sullivan epitomizes psychotherapy in the following manner: One person, the therapist, is designated an expert in interpersonal relationships and emotional functioning, and the other, who may be called the patient, client or inter-

viewee, needs help in these areas; they come together in a set professional situation to meet these needs.

Psychotherapy, Sullivan states, is the hardest work he knows, and he spent his childhood and adolescence doing manual labor on his father's farm. Psychotherapy requires continuous vigilance, flexibility, and ingenuity by the therapist, and there is no fun in it. The therapist who feels that he can relax or enjoy the process simply does not know what he is doing. Enthusiasm about psychotherapy, by either the therapist or the patient, is absurd. It indicates immaturity on the part of one or both of them, or little comprehension of what psychotherapy is all about.

Sullivan emphasizes that there is no such person as a "neutral" therapist, acting as if he and the patient had never met each other. The therapist is always emotionally involved to some extent in the interview. Anxiety occasionally is aroused in him and his vanity is from time to time gratified or abashed. His sympathy is sometimes stimulated, his irritability is at times provoked, and he now and then is either bored or fascinated by patients. The therapist must, of course, work hard to keep such emotional reactions to a minimum, for, inevitable as they are, they constitute barriers to understanding the patient and comprehending what is occurring in the interview. A strong emotional response in the therapist cripples him so long as it lasts, and in some cases constitutes a psychiatric problem. It is this continuous struggle to be an alert observer, participating in the interview but only minimally involved in it emotionally, that, among other things, makes psychotherapy arduous work.

On the other hand, the therapist must have a con-

stant, intense interest in the patient as someone who needs his help; indifference to the patient is disastrous.

In his interaction with the patient it is imperative that the therapist abandon all interest in the ordinary satisfactions of interpersonal relationships. He must not expect pleasure, gratitude, friendship, or any other gratification which he might get in other kinds of interpersonal activity. He does not seek prestige or admiration or any other type of emotional support from the patient. His job is to help the patient understand himself, and his only satisfactions come from exercising his best possible professional skill and being reasonably well paid for it. His only emotional gratification should be that of a craftsman who is doing his job as well as he knows.

The therapist must, however, have a high degree of respect for the patient; he must at all times view the patient as someone worthy of his continuous, alert willingness to help. This respect is based not on any particular qualities the patient has as an individual, but on the nature and aims of the patient-therapist relationship. As part of this respect, the therapist is at all times attentive to what the patient, verbally and nonverbally, is communicating; the therapist is continually sensitive to the patient's anxiousness, perplexity, and emotional comfort or discomfort. The therapist also must realize that the patient is constantly scrutinizing him; he is examining the impact that each thing he says and does has on the therapist.

A large part of the participant observation in which the therapist and patient engage is focused on examination of the two-person interpersonal field that is

automatically set up in the interview. In addition to investigating events in the patient's past and current life situations, they examine what is going on in the interview relationship itself, for it usually is the only sample of the patient's interpersonal life that is available for direct scrutiny. The therapist and the patient can explore how the patient reacts to the therapist, how he attempts to manipulate the therapist, what he expects of the therapist, and many other things. From examination of this specimen of the patient's interpersonal activity much often can be learned about his other past and present interpersonal relationships.

Sullivan recommends that a therapist take notes only during the first two or three interviews; these initial sessions often are devoted to making a broad, superficial survey of the patient's past and current life situations. The therapist can explain note-taking briefly by saying, "During the first two or three sessions I usually take notes while I am learning the basic facts about who a patient is and what has happened to him during his life. I simply can't remember details such as how many brothers and sisters he has, where he went to school, and so forth, without notes. After that, as we begin to explore what has gone on, and is going on, between the patient and other people, I no longer take notes. We're far too busy for that."

If a therapist takes notes after the first two or three interviews, one of two things occurs: Either the notes are so badly written and poorly organized that they are of little use to the therapist, or the therapist's concentration on his note-taking destroys the vitality of the patient-therapist relationship and impairs the work at hand.

Sullivan feels that this interpersonal approach to psychotherapy offers hope that in time psychotherapy can become a truly scientific discipline in which principles, techniques, and results can be objectively evaluated and verified. He feels that it thus will be removed from the sphere of personal testimonials and airy speculations, and that the master-to-apprentice mode of training psychotherapists will be abandoned. He realizes, however, that this goal will require decades of detailed study of psychotherapy from many points of view.

## THE PROCEDURES AND TACTICS OF PSYCHOTHERAPY

Psychotherapy is composed of five basic processes.

1. *Examination of current or recently past interpersonal relationships, especially with those persons with whom the patient has had relatively durable associations.* This involves detailed evaluation of his interactions with the persons with whom he lives, the people with whom he works and associates socially, and any others with whom he has emotionally significant contacts.

2. *Exploration of the patient's relationships with people in his past life.* This includes his relationships with his parents, siblings, close childhood and adolescent friends, sexual partners, work associates, and others with whom he has been emotionally close. This category, like the first one, also may embrace socioeconomic aspects of the patient's life; for example, it may involve examination of how academic and voca-

tional successes and failures have influenced his relationships with people.

3. *Attention to any immediate interpersonal crises in the patient's life.* Such crises offer the patient and the therapist fresh, emotionally charged material with which to work. Hence they may be particularly useful to explore, especially if they can be linked to previous such dilemmas.

4. *Discussion of future interpersonal relationships.* Sullivan is unique, among psychotherapeutic pioneers, in his preoccupation with the future as well as the present and the past. He advocates examination of the future by what he calls "constructive revery." In essence, the therapist says to the patient, "Let us examine your free-flowing speculations about where these interpersonal events and relationships are heading. Where are they taking you? For example, what do you feel the nature of your relationship with your marital partner will be in a month, or a year, or ten years?" Consideration of the patient's apprehensions, expectations, and other feelings about the future can in many cases open up important therapeutic areas.

5. *Exploration of the patient-therapist relationship.* As pointed out above, this is usually the only interpersonal relationship of the patient that is available for direct examination during a course of psychotherapy.

In the following pages many aspects of these five basic processes in therapy will be covered. The interviewer's task is to discover, in all senses, who the patient is. He must establish what the patient's problems in living are, how they arose out of past interpersonal associations, and how they are expressed in current interactions with people. The therapist should explore

how the patient's difficulties distort his expectations of the future. Although there are no universal rules about how a patient acquires insight, it usually begins with awareness of small things in his day-to-day life and proceeds to awareness of larger things from his past. Psychotherapy requires meticulous attention to detail, unflagging vigilance, and willingness to explore all aspects of any facet of the patient's life.

## THE ORGANIZATION OF AN INTERVIEW

Every interview should follow, at least roughly, a well-conceived plan; every series of interviews should do so also. Though the therapist is quite flexible, he never allows therapy to jolt along in a purposeless, haphazard manner. The therapist is not certain where he and the patient are going, but he knows that their therapeutic venture must have a beginning, an itinerary, and an end.

Sullivan feels that each interview, and every course of psychotherapy, should be composed of four basic parts: (1) the *inception*, (2) the *reconnaissance*, (3) the *detailed inquiry*, and (4) the *termination*, or *interruption*.

The use of this four-part scheme in organizing psychotherapy is illustrated by the following brief example.

(1) At the *inception* of an interview a patient states that during the preceding two days he has been upset by problems between himself and his marital partner. As a rule the therapist does not allow him to drop this topic after a few moments; he also does not permit him

203

to ramble endlessly in repetitive, nonproductive ways about it. the therapist seeks to understand the nature, causes, and consequences of these interpersonal problems and to help the patient develop greater awareness about them.

Hence, by his comments and questions the therapist begins (2) the *reconnaissance*. What is the general nature of these tensions between the patient and his marital partner? When and how did they begin? Exactly what happens, step by step, during an interpersonal conflict about them? What kinds of further difficulties do these conflicts produce?

The reconnaissance (which is, of course, much more extensive than these few questions would indicate) passes imperceptibly into (3) the *detailed inquiry*. On this particular occasion what did your marital partner say? What did you reply? I don't understand; what do you mean by "upset"? Has this sort of difficulty arisen between the two of you previously, and, if so, what happened on some of these occasions? In this manner the reconnaissance and the detailed inquiry may last from fifteen minutes to many interviews, depending on the area under discussion. A large part of therapy, whether in a single interview or a prolonged course of psychotherapy, occurs during the phases of reconnaissance and detailed inquiry.

At the end of each detailed inquiry a specific (4) *termination* occurs. Each interview, and each course of therapy, should conclude in a carefully structured way. The patient expects some benefit from an interview and he should be given something to carry away from it, even if it is no more than the crystallization of a feeling or the clarification of some minor feature of

his customary mode of relating to people. The patient should not go away empty-handed. Sullivan feels this is a practical, as well as a therapeutic, necessity. For example, in the case of the patient who is discussing a marital conflict, the therapist at the end of the detailed inquiry, however short or long, should point out unnoticed feelings, aspects of the conflict of which the patient has been unaware, or ways in which the patient is carrying into his marital relationship patterns of interaction he developed earlier in his life. If the detailed inquiry goes on for several interviews, some kind of insight, however limited, should be offered him at the end of each session.

In concluding an important phase of treatment the termination sometimes is fairly detailed. It may include a summary of what has been learned, a prescription for some kind of limited action in regard to a problem, an assessment of the probable effects of these things on the patient's life situation, and many other kinds of things.

Sullivan employs this four-part organization of material in yet another way. He feels that before psychotherapy begins the therapist should make a systematic, careful evaluation of a patient to determine whether he should have psychotherapy. Psychotherapy is not for everyone; some people have little chance of benefit from it and others may be badly damaged. A therapist does not know whether psychotherapy is more likely to help or harm a patient unless he has evaluated him thoroughly before beginning it. Sullivan recommends from two or three to a dozen interviews for such an evaluation, using the four-part scheme outlined above. In his book *The Psychiatric*

*Interview* he described this pretherapy evaluation in detail. The patient, of course, often benefits from this evaluation, regardless of whether it is followed by systematic psychotherapy. He may experience some relief and acquire a certain degree of insight.

### THE THINGS THE THERAPIST SAYS AND DOES

The therapist's actions vary much from patient to patient, and often from one interview to the next. They vary depending on how well patients can talk about different subjects, how important the subjects are, and how deeply they need be, or can be, investigated. In some interviews the therapist is silent much of the time, only inserting a question or a comment now and then. In others he is busy most of the time in an ongoing exploratory dialogue with the patient.

The therapist often says things to center the patient's attention on the nub of the matter at hand. For example, he may say, "It appears that your main feeling during this conflict was *fear* of what he would do." The therapist frequently asks if the patient has omitted things in accounts he has given: "Did either of you mention the children while you were discussing this?" He may inquire if an action was perhaps meant to have a certain effect: "Do you think that by those actions your parents conveyed their feelings that your sister was more capable and worthwhile than you?"

The therapist at times may inquire if some detail can be recalled which would indicate that a previously unrecognized end was sought: "When you left the apartment did you take all your things with you, or did you,

perhaps unintentionally, leave things behind that you would later have to return to get?" Following up this question, the therapist may ask, "Is it possible, then, that you really did not intend to make a complete break?" The therapist often asks what the patient felt other people's motives were: "What did you feel their motives were when they did that, and have you since then changed your mind about their intentions?"

Sullivan does not hesitate to use directed (or "loaded") questions, provided certain precautions are taken. Directed questions on occasion have particular value. For example, it may be more effective to ask, "Do you feel she was becoming more irritable toward you?" than to say, "She was becoming more irritable toward you." A questions leads the patient's attention more forcefully to the point at hand since it requires a response, and the response, in turn, opens the way to more questions or comments.

A directed question, moreover, helps both the therapist and the patient to focus their attention on a specific topic, or on some aspect of it. It is the difference between saying, "Turn on your flashlight" and "Shine your flashlight in that corner." For example, if the therapist asks an undirected question such as "How did he react to that?" the patient may simply reply, "I don't know" or "I can't recall." The matter, which may be an important one, dies unless the therapist proceeds to ask directed questions: "Did he seem saddened by it?" "Did he seem a little frightened by it?" "Is it possible that he was more annoyed than anything else?" The important precaution in employing directed questions is to ask enough of them to explore *all aspects* of a topic and *all possible meanings* of an event. By a

long series of questions, some directed and some not, the therapist and patient examine a topic or event from many points of view until a thorough comprehension of it is achieved.

On many occasions the therapist and the patient jointly examine the evidence for something the patient believes. For example, the therapist may ask a patient what evidence there is that someone in his life has a particular personality quality which the patient sees in him: "What sorts of things does she say and do which make you think she is emotionally cold?" "What kinds of things does he do that make you feel he is hostile toward everyone and not just toward you?"

The therapist should not ask questions simply to keep the interview going; his task is to discover in a mutual venture with the patient what happened, why it happened, and what it meant. A good interview is busy and fast-moving. Sullivan stresses that there is no time to waste in psychotherapy; the therapist should not allow the patient to digress into trivialities and repetitions.

*The therapist should never assume that he knows what the patient is talking about.* He doesn't know until he and the patient have thoroughly explored the matter at hand. The most common error in all types of psychotherapy is presumption by the therapist that he understands something which in fact he does not. The meaning of something is not clear until it has been extensively investigated. For example, if a therapist reported in a case conference, "At this point the patient's mother left the room, and this is one more instance of her characteristic rejection of him when he was in any way assertive," Sullivan would inquire, "What is the

evidence that in leaving the room at that moment she was rejecting him?" "What did she say?" "What was her facial expression?" "Did she use any particular gesture?" "Did the doorbell ring just before she left?" "Even though it is clear that she often did reject him when he was assertive, what is the evidence that she so rejected him on this occasion?"

*You don't know until you find out,* Sullivan insists, and if you assume you know when you really don't, you and the patient are engaged in a pointless venture. Moreover, by misunderstanding the patient you may mislead and damage him.

A therapist should select those things he does well in interviews and build his psychotherapeutic repertory out of them. Each therapist, by trial and error and by gradual growth in his craft, selects the techniques best suited to him. Sullivan, for example, was often melodramatic in therapy. To express skepticism about something he would remove his glasses, stare at a patient, and say, "Extraordinary!" For other purposes, he would say, "My God! Tell me all about it," or, "Good Lord! How did that happen?" To reassure a patient about guilt over masturbation, Sullivan would sigh and say wearily, "Don't tell me you're another one of those people who feel their whole lives have been ruined by masturbation."

The value of many of the therapist's comments and communications is delayed. Often a patient receives an interpretation with polite acquiescence, but it means nothing to him until days, weeks, or months later when he integrates it into a vivid experience. He "discovers it" himself, unaware of its previous formulation in an interview.

Much of the communication in an interview, perhaps more than half of it, is nonverbal. Both the patient and the therapist convey much information by their facial expressions, gestures, and other wordless acts. The therapist must be alert to pick up as many as possible of these nonverbal clues. Also, he should in deliberate ways use his facial expressions, intonations, and gestures to transmit information to the patient. A skeptical wrinkling of the brow, a reassuring tone of voice, or a puzzled palm-upward gesture may be much more effective than words in getting a point across.

*A person achieves emotional health to the extent that he becomes aware of his interpersonal relationships.* Sullivan frequently uses this statement in response to questions from patients such as "What is wrong with me?" "What are we trying to accomplish in therapy?" and "How can I improve?" He feels that this answer, in addition to being valid, points to the general direction that therapy should take and opens wide areas for exploration. He views this statement as the thesis which holds therapy together; it weaves all questions, statements, and interpretations into a single fabric. He also views it as a succinct expression of the nature of the curative change in psychotherapy.

## ANXIETY AND SELECTIVE INATTENTION IN PSYCHOTHERAPY

The work of psychotherapy is constantly hindered by the patient's *anxiety* and *security operations.* Sullivan employs the term *anxiety* (Chapter 2) to designate a wide spectrum of painful feelings and emotion-

al forces; it includes anxiousness, guilt, shame, dread, panic, and other forms of emotional distress. As the patient talks about his problems he feels anxiousness, guilt, and other uncomfortable sensations when painful subjects are approached. Hence, in ways of which he is largely unaware, the patient shies away from these topics; he veers into other areas or becomes silent.

The thing that prevents a person from changing is that at some time in the past he has learned that inquiry into, or knowledge of, some aspect of living is fraught with anxiety, danger, and discomfort, and that area of living is excluded from his awareness. A central process in therapy is the gradual focusing of the patient's attention on those interpersonal experiences, and exploration of how they have warped his personality and emotional functioning.

Sullivan employs the term *selective inattention* (Chapter 2) to designate the process by which a person deflects his attention from interpersonally painful areas of his life. Selective inattention is a major type of security operation; security operations (Chapter 2) are the characteristic techniques a person unawarely uses to avoid anxiety and keep his emotional comfort at a high level.

Selective inattention to some extent operates almost continually in each person's emotional life. To see all painful things, nakedly and bleakly, would be intolerable. *Each person, therefore, tends continually to restrict his focus of awareness to those things in his life which are comfortable and to eliminate from his field of attention those that are distressing.*

Selective inattention can be illustrated in the follow-

ing simple example. In a marital relationship each person by selective inattention avoids stark confrontation with many of the shortcomings of his partner. He/she does not see many signs of irritability, crudeness, and boredom, but constricts attention to one's partner's affectionate, talented, and interesting qualities. If each marital partner's defects are minor and can in general be overlooked by selective inattention, or can be disguised by some other nondamaging security operation, the marriage goes well. It goes well because selective inattention shields each marital partner from many of the defects of the other. This is seen most clearly in a newly met, infatuated couple; they often cannot see glaring defects in each other.

If, however, a marital partner's imperfections are so large and disturbing that they cannot be screened out by selective inattention, one of two things will happen. The person will either become aware of his partner's shortcomings, and will experience much emotional pain in the process, or he will begin to use various security operations to remain unaware of his partner's defects. In the latter case he may develop a sick view of his marriage; he may view his partner's brutality as his "strength," or his fearfulness as his "cautiousness and prudence,"or his coldness as his "dignity."

*Dealing with the patient's selective inattention to many painful aspects of past and current interpersonal relationships is a major, almost constant task of psychotherapy.* Selective inattention operates throughout therapy in a smooth, seemingly impervious manner, hiding from the patient (and often the therapist) innumerable things and making their investigation

difficult. A continual task of therapy is (1) to discover how selective inattention is affecting the patient's ability to explore the subject at hand and (2) to identify and deal with the kind of anxiety that is causing selective inattention to operate at that moment.

This is made clear in an elementary example. In talking about his relationship with his parents, a patient states that during his adolescence his parents were very concerned that he associate with the right kinds of adolescents. An alert therapist does not leave this statement unexamined. He inquires about the exact ways in which they expressed their concern that he associate only with "the right kinds of adolescents." What were their criteria for acceptable friends? What do these criteria tell us about his parents? What do they tell us about the patient, who accepted them? Did the patient consider these criteria reasonable at the time, and does he now in retrospect consider them reasonable? In what ways did his parents' criteria about acceptable associates for him restrict his social life during his adolescence? Did their stringent criteria in fact constitute rationalizations to keep him tied to themselves? Did they have a need to dominate him? Were they, because of their personality difficulties, overly possessive of him? Did they have a need to keep him bound to them in an immature role?

The therapist and patient go on to investigate whether other people, by their comments at the time, indicated that they viewed his parents' attitudes as possessive, domineering, and self-centered. Did the same thing go on during his earlier years in his relationship with them? Do these attitudes of his parents still persist, even though he is an adult? In brief, *how has se-*

*lective inattention operated throughout his life to keep him from seeing a significant aspect of his interpersonal relationships?* The ramifications of this subject could occupy the patient and the therapist in several, or perhaps many, interviews.

In this illustration selective inattention *also* operated between the patient and the therapist *during the interview.* In the interview situation the patient was at first unable to see, because of selective inattention, what he had not seen during many years of his life; these things remained obscure until selective inattention was removed by the therapist's professional skills. This is one of the things that makes psychotherapy a unique interpersonal experience; *it is the only interpersonal relationship in the person's life in which a systematic, deliberate attempt is made to stop the operation of selective inattention and to help the patient include in his experience many things he previously excluded.*

Sullivan repeatedly emphasizes that *a person cannot discuss and emotionally assimilate a thing he has not experienced, and if something has been excluded from his awareness by selective inattention he has not experienced it.* For example, the man cited in the illustration above had never *experienced* his parents' possessiveness and domination of him since selective inattention had kept it out of his focus of awareness. Since he had never experienced it, he had been unable to deal with it in a healthy way. *Therapy to a large extent consists of broadening a person's experience by bringing into his focus of attention many things of which he previously had been unaware and therefore unable to resolve in a healthy way.*

214

To accomplish this the therapist must deal with the patient's anxiety—his anxiousness, guilt, feelings of inadequacy, and other forms of emotional distress which he feels when he confronts these things. Nonverbal techniques are as important as verbal ones in dealing with this anxiety. The therapist's obvious lack of alarm, censure, and disgust as the patient discusses painful areas of his life are as important as what he says; in some instances the therapist's reassurance is conveyed mainly by nonverbal means. By its very nature the therapist's attitude says, "There are no valid reasons for you to feel anxious, guilty, and inadequate. The things we are discussing are merely experiences we must examine to solve your interpersonal and emotional problems."

In addition, of course, the therapist crystallizes his anxiety-relieving measures in words. He says, in essence, "You have long been upset about this. You have been anxious in talking about it here. However, as we examine this area of your interpersonal life we can see that your distress about it is not justified; it is an emotional problem which we are trying to resolve by investigating this subject in many contexts and from many points of view. When you see it fully, and understand what has occurred, and why it has happened, it will lose its painfulness for you."

Sullivan often used rhetorical, emphatic questions in dealing with anxiety: "Well, and what is really so wrong about that?" "Why are you so concerned about such a common thing?" "What is so lamentable, or difficult, about this?" He once stated that psychotherapy with disturbed adolescents consists mainly of finding out what is supposed to be so terrible, and then

showing by what one says and does that it is not terrible at all. This is an oversimplification, but it is a striking way of making an important point.

*Selective inattention also creates interpersonal barriers between the patient and the therapist.* The patient is continually fending off the therapist; he fights abandonment of selective inattention, and he avoids coming to grips with painful aspects of his life. The patient is an unwilling ally in the work to which he and the therapist have set themselves, *for what they discuss is often painful to the patient and rarely so to the therapist.* Thus the therapist must constantly be hard at work helping the patient to deal with his anxiety.

### EXAMINATION OF THE PATIENT-THERAPIST RELATIONSHIP

As has been noted briefly above, there is during psychotherapy only one interpersonal relationship available for direct examination, the relationship between the patient and the therapist; it is hence a particularly valuable one to observe and investigate.

In a course of extended psychotherapy the patient often begins to treat the therapist *as if he were someone from his past life;* that is, the patient develops a *parataxic distortion* (Chapter 3) about the therapist. For example, a patient who throughout his childhood and adolescence had a harsh, mutually hostile relationship with his father may begin to react toward the therapist *as if he were his father;* he becomes defiant, fearful, and competitive toward the therapist. He is carrying into the patient-therapist relationship the un-

healthy interpersonal patterns he had in his relationship with his father.

The patient has, of course, carried this distorted interpersonal pattern into many other areas of his life. He has expressed it in relationships with male superiors in his academic career, vocational activities, social life, and other spheres. In ways he does not understand, he repeatedly is trying to solve old problems in new situations by reliving them; he unawarely is seeking to work them out and establish better patterns for relating to people. The victim is always returning to the scenes of the crimes that were committed against him.

There is an important difference between the patient's parataxic distortions in his social life and in his relationship with the therapist. In his social, vocational, and other interpersonal activities his parataxic distortions cause strong emotional reactions in the people with whom he becomes involved. They become angry, frightened, disgusted, or puzzled by his actions. They argue with him, censure him, or abandon him in disgust or bewilderment. They feel that his behavior is personally directed at them, or conclude that he is a troublesome, undesirable person with whom to associate. If they make any effort at all to understand him they do so only in terms of their immediate relationship with him; they do not see his behavior as part of a broader pattern with old roots in his earlier life experiences. Understanding him is not their job. An employer, teacher, or social acquaintance has neither the time nor the training to try to change a parataxic distortion in him, and the person himself is not oriented toward doing it in a social relationship.

The therapist does not react emotionally to the patient; instead, he treats the patient's behavior as important material for the therapeutic process and makes as much use as possible of it. The therapist asks, "Where does this parataxic distortion come from? Who is the other person with whom the patient is emotionally confusing me? What happened in his relationship with that other person? How can we use this material to broaden the patient's awareness of what has gone on, and is going on, in his interpersonal life?"

The first demonstration of a parataxic distortion in therapy is often unsettling to the patient. It may mobilize a certain amount of anxiety in him. Having outlined the nature of the parataxic distortion, the therapist indicates that it must have a history, and that it must be connected with the patient's relationship with some significant, close person in his past life. In the case of adolescents and children this person may be someone in his current life situation. The therapist says, in essence: Let us explore its origin and examine all aspects of it. Let us see how it is causing you much trouble in your present interpersonal associations. The identification of the first parataxic distortion is often a milestone in therapy.

Sullivan has a striking way of talking about parataxic distortions. He says that, sooner or late, an "imaginary" or "illusory" person becomes involved in the two-person, patient-therapist relationship. Three people are then present in the interview—the patient, the therapist, and the person from the patient's past. Putting the matter somewhat differently, Sullivan says that the three persons present in the interview are the patient; the observing, actual psychiatrist; and the

imaginary, parataxic psychiatrist. The job of the observing, actual psychiatrist is gradually to eliminate the imaginary, parataxic psychiatrist by finding out where he comes from and how he disturbs the patient's life.

Looking at patient-therapist relationships from yet another angle (and it is the essence of Sullivanian psychiatry to look at everything from as many angles as possible), the patient and the therapist are much of the time examining the *field of interaction* involving the two of them. This is at times a cooperative social field. At other times it is a parataxically distorted one. At still other times it is a conflict-laden field in which a sensitive therapist is attempting to help an anxious patient to examine subjects that upset him. Sullivan feels strongly that comprehensive observation of this *field of interaction* offers hope that in time it can be studied, not only by the therapist and the patient, but also by neutral third parties who can verify or contradict the therapist's concepts of what is occurring in it. This will enable psychotherapy slowly to evolve from a ritual-filled art into a truly scientific discipline.

A patient may make several parataxic distortions during a long course of therapy, and identification and exploration of them is one of the most difficult tasks of psychotherapy. The therapist must be careful not to become emotionally embroiled in these parataxic distortions. As an example of this, Sullivan points out the following sequence of events: A therapist becomes irritable, or discouraged, or bored with a patient who taunts him, or does not improve, or talks repetitively on the same topics. The psychiatrist conceals these feelings from himself, and perhaps from others, by

pinning pessimistic diagnostic labels on the patient. He says that the patient "has a psychotic core that previously was not apparent, and that because of it it is doubtful that he can work through his problems," or that "his paranoid (or psychopathic) nucleus is now evident, and he is not a candidate for deep therapy ." The therapist often adds that "the most we can hope for in this case is reconstitution of the patient's fragmented ego so that he can regain his former level of marginal social adjustment." Although such statements are sometimes valid, they more often are devious ways of saying, "I am irritated, or discouraged, or bored by this patient, and I am going to send him packing." Sullivan did not engage in such frauds and was impatient with others who did so.

There is no standard pattern for psychotherapy. However, it usually moves from examination of current interpersonal relationships to investigation of old ones. Exploration of the patient-therapist relationship is, with some notable exceptions, a late development.

In some cases, contrary to the statement just made, the patient's parataxic distortion toward the therapist creates such marked obstacles in therapy that it must be handled early in treatment. This is illustrated in the following example: In the context of his relationships with domineering, guilt-manipulating parents and other close persons, a patient has evolved into a passive, apprehensive, ingratiating person who behaves in an appeasing, flattering manner toward everyone. He is so anxious to avoid saying or doing anything that might displease the therapist that he cannot discuss anything of significance in his interviews. His parataxic distortion is so severe that effective therapy is im-

possible until it is at least partially resolved. The therapist must identify this parataxic distortion, show how it is obstructing therapy, and trace out at least superficially some of its roots. During the subsequent course of therapy he in many cases must deal repeatedly with this parataxic distortion when, under the stress of anxiety, the patient puts up this barrier again and again to avoid exploring painful aspects of his life.

# 7

## Sullivan's Methods of Psychotherapy: Further Features

### THE NATURE OF THE PSYCHOTHERAPEUTIC CURE

LIKE MOST psychiatrists, Sullivan sometimes quibbles about the use of the word "cure" in psychiatry. He recognizes that all people suffer a certain amount of emotional distress from time to time and have at least minor personality problems and interpersonal difficulties. Hence a psychiatrist or other mental health professional worker does not cure interpersonal and emotional problems in the same sense that a nonpsychiatric physician cures a broken ankle or pneumonia. However, once the limitations of the word "cure" are made clear, Sullivan uses it as the simplest term to designate what the therapist and patient are striving for in their therapeutic venture.

The concept of the psychotherapeutic cure may be considered by examining six statements about it:

(1) *A person who has an emotional problem has it because in some way he has been restrained from using the totality of his powers.*

(2) *The elimination of parataxic distortions is a major goal of psychotherapy.*

(3) *In psychotherapy the patient gradually abandons unhealthy security operations.*

(4) *Planned, systematic consensual validation is a central aspect of the psychotherapeutic process.*

(5) *A person has awareness, and understanding, of his experience only to the extent that he has formulated it in communication to another person, or has crystallized it to himself in articulate, reflective thinking.*

(6) *A person achieves emotional health to the extent that he becomes aware of his interpersonal relationships.*

By inspecting each of these six statements in some detail a fairly clear concept of the psychotherapeutic cure may be achieved.

(1) *A person who has an emotional problem has it because in some way he has been restrained from using the totality of his powers.* In accordance with his concepts of the *tendency toward health* (Chapter 2) and the *one-genus postulate* (Chapter 3), Sullivan feels that an individual spontaneously moves toward emotional health once the obstacles to such progress are removed. In the active sense of the word, a therapist never "cures" anybody. He only removes obstacles, and the patients thereafter cure themselves. The principal task of the therapist is "brush-clearing"; once the obstructing brush has been cleared the plants which the brush has been stunting grow robustly.

This principle is illustrated in the three following examples. A person who has a passive personality disorder is unable to be assertive. He allows others to dominate and exploit him, and is on an endless treadmill to secure their approval and affection by deference to them. The underlying problem of this patient

is not his passivity; it is the marked anxiety he feels when he is in the least way aggressive. He dreads that others will become angry and reject him if he is assertive, and he feels that their anger and rejection will be proof that he is the inadequate, worthless person he fears he is. At the root of his passivity are profound feelings of inadequacy and worthlessness. The task of therapy is therefore to resolve this patient's feelings of inadequacy and worthlessness, thus eliminating his panic when others become angry at him. When he no longer dreads the possibility of other people's anger and rejection he will develop the capacity to be assertive in comfortable, reasonable ways. In other words, when the obstacles to assertiveness are removed the patient "cures himself" by abandoning his passivity.

The main task in treating a schizoid person is not to deal with his social isolation and lack of close relationships with people. The patient's central difficulty is his profound conviction (of which he often is only dimly aware) that all interpersonal relationships are painful and menacing, and that uninvolvement in them is the only safe course. If the therapist can remove the patient's dread of interaction with people and his anxiety whenever he begins to get close to anyone, the patient proceeds to "cure himself" by forming sound associations with people.

Similarly, the therapeutic task in treating a homosexual, Sullivan states, lies not in dealing with his homosexual acts and relationships, but in removing his deep distrust and apprehensiveness about closeness, and especially genital-to-genital contact, with persons of the opposite sex. When this dread has been removed the person no longer seeks homosexual partners, but

gradually becomes comfortable in channeling his sexual yearnings in heterosexual directions.

(2) *The elimination of parataxic distortions is a major goal of psychotherapy.* An emotionally healthy individual does not in distorted ways treat people in his current relationships as if they were persons from his past life. For example, a healthy man does not flee from closeness with women because in each woman he fears the harshness and painful domination he had in his relationship with his mother; a healthy woman does not behave similarly with men. A well-adjusted individual can deal with a person in his current life according to that person's merits; his relationship with that person is not distorted by what Sullivan calls "illusory" or "imaginary" persons from the individual's past.

In therapy such parataxic distortions (Chapter 3) are handled in two ways. Firstly, the patient and the therapist examine how they are affecting many of the patient's day-to-day relationships with people. Secondly, they explore how in time the patient sets up a parataxic distortion in his relationship with the therapist. This latter subject has been dealt with in detail in the preceding chapter.

(3) *In psychotherapy the patient gradually abandons the use of unhealthy security operations.* Security operations (Chapter 2) are interpersonal maneuvers to decrease anxiety. Security operations may be healthy or unhealthy, and the identification and removal of unhealthy ones is an important facet of the psychotherapeutic cure.

The following case vignette illustrates in a simple way the operation and removal of an unhealthy securi-

ty operation. A woman in her second marriage is obsessively concerned about the welfare of her five-year-old son, whom she had in a previous unhappy marriage. When he is out of sight she worries that he has been injured in an accident, has become suddenly ill, or has had some other type of mishap. Her fearful preoccupation about him is an obvious personality problem; it causes many difficulties in her relationship with her son and with her current husband, with whom she is otherwise well adjusted. Psychotherapeutic examination of this mother's unhealthy closeness to her son reveals that she is carrying over to him much of the bitterness she feels toward her first husband, whom the boy strongly resembles physically and whose name he bears. Unable to face her guilt-ridden feelings of rejection and hostility toward her son, she is engaging in an unhealthy security operation; she covers her hostility by adopting an overt attitude which is precisely its opposite. It is as if she were saying, in essence, "I do not have hostile feelings toward my son. On the contrary, I am continually concerned about his well-being and safety." The elimination of this unhealthy security operation, of which she is unaware and into which she has no insight, is an important goal of the psychotherapy which she undergoes to increase her own emotional comfort and stop the personality damage she is inflicting on her son.

The psychiatric cure as a rule requires the exploration and resolution of various unhealthy security operations and the substitution of sound interactional patterns in their places.

(4) *Systematic consensual validation is a central aspect of the psychotherapeutic process.* Consensual val-

idation (Chapter 3) is the process by which a person arrives at a *consensus* with another individual about some aspect of his feelings, thoughts, or interpersonal relationships, and *validates* that consensus by repeated examinations of it in many kinds of experiences.

As pointed out in Chapter 3, consensual validation is the basic process by which a person forms concepts of himself and of interpersonal relationships and his roles in them. In day-to-day life consensual validations occur spontaneously; that is, they occur in unplanned ways of which the person is not articulately aware. In psychotherapy, however, consensual validation is employed as a deliberate, planned technique for enlarging a person's awareness of himself and his interpersonal life. All hypotheses in psychotherapy are repeatedly evaluated from many points of view by the patient and the therapist until consensual validations about them are achieved.

The operation of consensual validation is sometimes explained by use of the following metaphor: If a person views a statue in semidarkness and from the front side only, he has an imperfect, often erroneous concept of it. If, however, in company with another person, he examines the statue with light falling on it from many different angles, looks at it both from a distance and up close, and passes his hand over its surface, he gradually develops a thorough comprehension of it; moreover, if throughout this time he discusses the statue with his companion and they compare their impressions, his understanding of it becomes still more extensive. He thus acquires a *consensually validated* concept of the statue.

The consensual validation that occurs in the inter-

view situation is supplemented by other consensual validations in the patient's daily life as his newly gained insights help him to see and understand more about what is going on in his relationships with people. He thus consolidates his progress in the context of his everyday living. His interpersonal life, in a sense, becomes the laboratory in which he continues to test what he has discovered in therapy, until his gains become integral parts of his personality structure.

(5) *A person has awareness, and understanding, about his experience only to the extent that he has formulated it in communication to another person, or has crystallized it to himself in articulate, reflective thinking.* Sullivan recognizes, indeed emphasizes, that much improvement in psychotherapy occurs by nonverbal means and that some patients make significant progress in solving interpersonal problems without clear formulations of the process in words. However, he feels that verbalization enhances such improvement and much increases the chances that it will be permanent. A person does not thoroughly understand his feelings and interpersonal relationships until he has expressed them in words. Much that some psychiatrists say is "repressed" is merely "unformulated and uncomunicated."

(6) *A person achieves emotional health to the extent that he becomes aware of his interpersonal relationships.* As noted in the preceding chapter, Sullivan feels that this statement constitutes a central thesis that binds together all aspects of the interpersonal approach to psychiatry. It encapsulates in a few words what is wrong with the patient, the aim of treatment, and the nature of the psychotherapeutic cure.

This statement also outlines the limitations of psychotherapy. When an individual's interpersonal problems are so deeply ingrained that he cannot develop awareness of them, psychotherapy offers him little. When awareness of his interpersonal difficulties arouses more anxiety in him than he can tolerate, and more turmoil than the therapist can assuage, psychotherapy is dangerous. When awareness threatens to destroy a patient's fragile adjustment and nothing workable can be put in its place, the aims of therapy must be severely curtailed.

## SULLIVAN'S OBJECTIONS TO FREUDIAN-PSYCHOANALYTIC THERAPY

Sullivan objected to various aspects of Freudian-psychoanalytic therapy, but we shall restrict our attention to three features of it about which Sullivan was most explicit. They are (1) *free association,* (2) *dream analysis,* and (3) *the process of noninterpersonal introspection.*

*Free Association.* In free association, the standard method employed in Freudian psychoanalysis, the patient is instructed to say without hesitation or inhibition everything that comes to mind. Freudian psychoanalysis holds that by this process of unconstrained speech the patient in time discovers the unconscious emotional traumas of the first seven years of his life that are causing his psychiatric problems.

Sullivan finds the concept of free association absurd. He says that in order truly to free associate a patient would have to have an impossibly low level of

anxiety. Hence, when a patient attempts to free associate he distorts everything related to his problems. His security operations cause him to give erroneous accounts of all aspects of his life that are disturbed by anxiety. As a result, one of two things happens: Either the patient talks only about those areas of his life in which he has few difficulties, or he talks about his problems in such oblique ways that no material of psychotherapeutic value emerges. To tell a patient to free associate, Sullivan states, is like saying to him, "Get rid of your anxiety and tell me about your fundamental problems." If the patient could do this he would not need psychotherapy.

A further defect in free association is that what the patient says is not further verified in an exploratory dialogue. Hypotheses are never tested by careful inquiry, evidence is always fragmentary, and the patient and the therapist never reach a well-examined conclusion about anything. Consensual validation never occurs.

*Dream Analysis.* Sullivan feels that although emotional problems are perhaps in some way reflected in dreams, it is impossible to discover what those problems are. This is owing to two factors. Firstly, the incomprehensible nature of the dream pictures, as remembered by the dreamer, indicates that any underlying meaning is obscured by elaborate camouflaging processes. Although many speculations may be made about how these camouflaging dream pictures are related to the patient's emotional forces and his past and current interpersonal life, there is no adequate method for determining if the speculations are valid. For the reasons cited in the two preceding paragraphs, free as-

sociation is not a reliable technique for testing the validity of such speculations. For example, if a person dreams that he is attacked by a bear, and a dream analyst says that this dream reveals fear of attack by his father, there is no scientific method for proving or disproving this hypothesis. Sullivan is skeptical, moreover, that any technique for accomplishing this task will ever be discovered. Belief in any system of dream interpretation is therefore a matter of faith, not science.

Secondly, Sullivan states, when a patient attempts to discover the hidden meaning of a dream he has a marked upsurge of anxiety, and this anxiety further distorts what he says about it. Hence, a patient and a therapist never deal with a dream itself; they talk only about recollections, thoughts, and speculations that are in some way related to the dream. The dream is beyond their reach, and the manner in which the patient's recollections and speculations are related to it is an insoluble problem.

A patient and a therapist can, of course, discuss the patient's dreams in the same manner in which they can discuss any other thought or speculation he has, and such discussions may reveal something about the patient's emotional and interpersonal life. However, they are not "analyzing" the dream. Discussion of distorted *recollections* of a dream is not "dream analysis."

By his irrefutable criticisms of free association and dream analysis Sullivan disturbed his Freudian-psychoanalytic colleagues in Washington, Baltimore, and New York, since free association and dream analysis are two of the fundamental processes in psychoanalysis (transference analysis is the third). Moreover, in-

validating these two investigative methods throws grave doubts on all the things Freud presumably discovered by their use. When the consequences of Sullivan's objections to Freudian psychoanalysis are grasped it is easy to see why conventional Freudian psychoanalysts were so hostile toward him during his lifetime and have continued so toward his viewpoints since his death.

*The Process of Noninterpersonal Introspection.* Sullivan distrusts prolonged introspection when it is not carried out in the context of a two-person dialogue. He feels that unguided, untested introspection produces such marked distortions because of the patient's anxieties and security operations that it is worse than useless. If such introspection occurs in psychotherapy the patient is often harmed by it, for he increases the number of his erroneous ideas about himself and his life.

Sullivan maintains that the introspection that occurs in Freudian psychoanalysis is unguided and untested since the therapist is silent the vast majority of the time. The therapist makes comments only occasionally, and the validity of his sparse interpretations is never tested out by systematic inquiry into them. Hence, the validity, or even the relevance, of the therapist's statements is never established.

Introspection is psychiatrically useful, Sullivan says, only when it occurs in an interpersonal setting. Its conclusions must be validated by extensive testing in a two-person dialogue with another individual who has much expertise in this kind of work. If a patient talks introspectively for long periods in the presence of a silent, unquestioning, unchecking therapist, as happens in classical Freudian psychoanalysis, he

veers away from anxiety-laden topics whenever he comes to them, or distorts them badly. Any theories constructed of material obtained in such psychotherapy will incorporate the common distortions and unsound ideas of patients into them. Moreover, there is no way, so long as the same method of gathering information is employed, by which these distortions and invalid ideas can be detected, let alone corrected. From decade to decade these errors will be taught by one generation of practitioners to the next.

*Psychotherapy, to be of value, must be an interpersonal process involving a patient and a therapist in a continually alert exploratory dialogue. All hypotheses must be examined, and in time validated, by investigating them repeatedly from many points of view.*

The popularity of Freudian psychoanalysis, Sullivan feels, arises from the fact that it offers its practitioners and patients a dogmatically set, secure ritual of treatment and an authoritarian body of theory which reassures both the therapist and the patient that at all times useful, sound things are being done. Sullivanian psychotherapy gives its practitioners and patients a much more difficult, less comforting task. It requires a continual, earnest, vibrant dialogue in which the therapist's expertise is constantly tested and the patient's anxiety is often mobilized.

Sullivan understands clearly the difficulties of the therapy he advocates. He says that a therapist who really comprehends the intimidating complexity of what he is doing soon realizes that his expertness is small and very defective. A self-assured, let alone arrogant, therapist simply does not understand what he is doing.

# THE DANGERS OF PSYCHOTHERAPY

Most distinguished innovators in psychiatry, in their enthusiasm to spread their points of view and acquire acceptance of them, have paid little attention to the dangers of psychotherapy. Though some of them have at times briefly noted that psychotherapy can damage as well as help patients, they have in general given little attention to this unpleasant subject in their eagerness to emphasize the possible benefits of their therapies. Sullivan faces these dangers bluntly and deals with them at length.

## PSYCHOTHERAPEUTIC FRAUD

One of the main dangers of psychotherapy, Sullivan points out, is that by nonverbal and verbal means the therapist may train the patient to say only the kinds of things that suit his theoretical prejudices.

Because of his intellectual and emotional investment in the particular psychiatric school of thought to which he adheres, the therapist encourages the patient to talk about some topics and discourages him from talking about others. Unaware of the fraud he is perpetrating on the patient, the therapist merely feels that he and the patient "must concentrate on relevant material." The therapist trains his patient by both verbal and nonverbal methods. He remains silent when the patient says things that are contrary to his theoretical prejudices, but makes interpretations and comments when the patient deals with material that confirms the

therapist's points of view. His voice is subtly indifferent, or bored, or impatient when the patient says things that jar his preconceptions, but it becomes slightly animated and encouraging when the patient says things that dovetail with his concepts. These maneuvers are, of course, camouflaged from both the patient and the therapist by psychiatric jargon; the therapist says, "The patient is beginning to work well in psychotherapy," and the patient says, "I am starting to talk about things that are relevant to my problems." In reality, they are simply talking about things that confirm the therapist's theoretical position.

Even when the therapist is silent most of the time he tends to communicate his feelings to the patient. He fidgets restlessly when some subjects are mentioned, but becomes alert when others are discussed. He jots notes when he feels the patient is talking about important items, but fiddles with his cigarette or pipe, or remains motionless, when he feels the patient is rambling in unprofitable areas. Even when the therapist sits out of sight, the patient can hear the faint rustling of paper, the soft scraping of a ballpoint pen, the picking up and laying down of a clipboard and other sounds which are exaggerated by the artificial quiet of a relatively soundless office.

After a few weeks or months of therapy a patient often becomes adept at searching the therapist's face to determine if he is pleased, or bored, or slightly annoyed. This may occur regardless of whether the patient and therapist sit face to face, for when the therapist sits out of sight he and the patient nevertheless face each other at the end of the hour, and the patient

can then note his apparent response to the content of the session.

In addition, therapists of all theoretical points of view occasionally say things that frankly encourage or discourage patients in talking about various subjects: "I think you have dealt with some meaningful things today." "We are entering a more productive phase of therapy." "Your transference feelings are causing you to veer away from the things that are troubling you." "You are bound to feel a bit uncomfortable, or even frankly anxious, when we discuss things that are related to your problems, as we have done today." If examined in grim honesty, many such statements mean, in essence, "At last you are beginning to talk about things that are congenial to my theoretical prejudices."

The therapist in time thus educates the patient to produce the kind of material he wants to hear, and still later to look at it from the therapist's points of view. This occurs regardless of whether the therapist's points of view are valid and relevant to the patient's difficulties. In this manner, Sullivan says, therapy may go on for long periods, or interminably, to the immense gratification of the therapist, and even to the satisfaction of the patient, but without effect on the patient's problem.

Moreover, it has been statistically shown that many people with emotional problems improve in time if they have no treatment at all. Stresses in their day-to-day lives decrease, social and economic tensions diminish, some types of problems become more tolerable as individuals pass from one age period to another, and many other poorly understood things occur

which cause improvements. If such improvement happens while a patient is in psychotherapy he almost invariably attributes his relief to the therapy; the therapist in most cases does likewise. Neither one considers the possibility that improvement merely occurred *during* therapy and not *because* of it. In occasional cases, Sullivan states somewhat acidly, when the patient has been sold a particularly troublesome bill of goods one must even consider the possibility that the patient improved *in spite of* therapy.

Sullivan feels that this to a large extent explains why therapists using diverse means of therapy and conflicting theoretical systems can find patients who seem to justify the validity of their points of view. A process of selection goes on. Many patients are referred to a particular therapist over a period of time; a sizable number of them, finding his treatment puzzling or unsuited to them, drop out of it. In time the therapist winnows through his patients until he has a case load of them who meet his theoretical and emotional needs. Sullivan describes this as a "cozy" situation for the therapist but a profitless one for his patients. Both the therapist and his patients are unaware of the humbug they are engaged in, and the therapist often advocates that aspirant therapists be trained to do what he is doing.

Moreover, it is a brave, rare patient who, after years of expensive treatment and personal inconvenience, can say to himself and others, "I wasted my time." Braver and rarer still is the therapist who after expensive, tedious years of training, and many more years of practice, and whose livelihood and social position to a large extent are based on his professional stance, can look sternly at his work and say, "I have been wrong."

Thus patients and therapists become joint conspirators in therapeutic misadventures.


## PSYCHOTHERAPEUTIC DAMAGE

Sullivan emphasizes that patients can be damaged as well as helped by psychotherapy. Probing panic-ridden areas of a patient's life can precipitate neurotic decompensation or a psychotic break, and such untoward events are more common than is often recognized. Sullivan is scornful of the ways in which therapists sometimes rationalize such damage to patients, or even proclaim that it is beneficial. He never uses terms such as "transference neurosis," "transference psychosis," and "unresolved transference feelings owing to the patient's premature termination of therapy."

One of Sullivan's axioms in therapy is: *Never undermine a patient's security (emotional comfort) unless you can offer something that will be promptly constructive.* The therapist should never allow the patient to suffer for long periods because as the result of therapy he has lost some aspect of his emotional security; this holds true even when the lost aspect of his emotional security was a sick one. The therapist should substitute something valid and reasonably comfortable in the place of whatever he takes away from the patient.

In his final lectures and seminars Sullivan repeatedly emphasizes the limitations of psychotherapy. He says that his experience has taught him that psychotherapy is not a panacea, that it has little to offer many patients, and that it can damage as well as help. Patients must be meticulously evaluated before treat-

ment to determine if psychotherapy has a reasonable chance of aiding them, and even in well-selected patients its results are often poor. In his last years Sullivan viewed psychotherapy with a frankness that is rare in people who have devoted their lives to it.

Toward the end of his life Sullivan placed much emphasis on a viewpoint he had had to some extent from his earliest period of psychiatric work. He said that hope for improved mental health of the public at large did not lie in one-to-one psychotherapy, or in group psychotherapy, but in the gradual reform of a social system which he viewed as pervasively sick in its attitudes and practices. So long as society as a whole was emotionally unhealthy, many persons reared in it would continue to be ill.

In his writings and lectures Sullivan frequently becomes vehement, even intemperate on this subject. He is keenly aware that his own unhappy childhood, turbulent adolescence, tawdry educational years, and lonely adulthood were to a large extent the product of the warps and inadequacies of the society in which he had been reared and had spent an often painful life.

Sullivan feels that all institutions, especially those that mold opinions and attitudes, should be mobilized in the broadest possible ways to alter gradually the unhealthy interpersonal environments that cause social distress and individual emotional problems. If psychiatric problems are caused by sick interpersonal environments they can be helped, and sometimes cured, by healthy ones. More important still, immense amounts of personal suffering and group conflict can be prevented by the eradication of diseased attitudes and customs.

At the time of his death Sullivan was beginning to outline broad plans for public education and the molding of social attitudes and opinions. He was spending much of his time attending conferences and organizing committees to work toward this admittedly distant goal. He died abruptly in Paris on his way back to America after attending a conference on this subject in Amsterdam.

# 8

## *The Relevance of the Psychiatry of Harry Stack Sullivan to Current American Dilemmas*

SULLIVAN felt strongly that the concepts of interpersonal psychiatry which he had developed were applicable to the solution of problems of large social and economic groups. In the terminal years of his life he had vague hopes that their use might even offer something to decreasing international tensions.

In this chapter we shall examine ways in which Sullivan's ideas might be employed to evaluate and resolve the problems of large groups of people. We shall investigate how his principles for understanding the interactions of two-person and several-person groups can be applied to the relationships of groups containing from hundreds of people to millions of people. None of the material in this chapter comes directly from Sullivan; it consists of extensions of his ideas to fields in which he was interested but did only limited work.

## RACIAL PROBLEMS

We shall first consider how Sullivan's ideas can be employed in understanding and perhaps resolving ra-

cial problems, and shall begin by examining a historical event, the Supreme Court's school desegregation decisions of 1954 and 1955.

The Supreme Court failed to hand down decisions that would lead to school desegregation. Rapid shifts of white people from city centers to distant suburbs, combined with other neighborhood regroupings since 1954, have left most blacks in mainly black schools and most whites in mainly white schools; most blacks still live in black neighborhoods and most whites still live in white neighborhoods. Other kinds of racial desegregation and civil liberties progress, such as vocational intermingling and voting franchise extension, have since 1950 been much more successful than school and neighborhood desegregation.

What went wrong?

In using Sullivan's principles, school desegregation must be viewed primarily as an *interpersonal* problem, rather than as a legal, or educational, or even moral one. It is a difficulty between two groups of people and centers on how they *feel* about each other and consequently interact. If progress can be made on how blacks and whites *feel* about each other, *think* about each other, and hence relate to each other, problems between them will be resolved more easily.

To a large extent, the Supreme Court based its school desegregation decision on psychological grounds. It held that separation of a large group of children and adolescents apart from all other children and adolescents, and placement of them in special schools on purely racial grounds, makes the segregated children feel inferior and despised. These children and adolescents consequently develop strong feelings of inadequacy which handicap them educationally

and emotionally, regardless of the quality of education that is offered them in their separate schools. Though this statement perhaps oversimplifies the court's decision, it contains the heart of the matter.

Looking at its decision from an *interpersonal* point of view, the court made a basic error. It did not consider the feelings and thoughts of *both* parties involved; it considered only the feelings and thoughts of the blacks. If a legal decision is to be made on largely psychological grounds, and if that decision is to be workable, it must give *equal* weight to the emotional states of both parties involved.

The court, of course, made limited concessons to white feelings because of long-established customs and traditions, as well as because of practical problems in implementing school desegregation. It ruled that desegregation need not be immediate; it was to proceed with "deliberate speed." The court's failure to balance its consideration of black psychology with a careful evaluation of white psychology is the primary cause of the debacle of its plans for school desegregation. A wiser court might have said: If this obviously unfair, cruel practice has gone on so long there must be *interpersonal* reasons for it, and successful desegregation must take these *interpersonal* reasons into account.

If Sullivan's principles are to be used, an important early step is to investigate how white people feel about black people, and in particular about white children attending school with black children. To get that information one must go as a *participant observer* into the communities involved. In Sullivan's words, a *reconnaissance* and a *detailed inquiry* must be made. By systematic individual and group interviews with per-

sons in the white community, by open hearings, by thorough canvassing of public opinion, and by other means, participant observers must investigate and gradually accumulate data about how people in the white community feel about black people and school desegregation.

The next step is to discover what the *anxieties* of the white people are in relation to black people (it must be kept in mind that Sullivan employs the term "anxiety" to designate a broad spectrum of uncomfortable feelings such as anxiousness, dread, guilt, and shame. If two groups of people remain rigidly apart from each other in circumstances in which a gradual mingling would be expected, a participant observer must ask: What anxieties are paralyzing communication between these two groups and are keeping them apart? In this particular case, what are the anxieties of the white people?

Studies employing Sullivan's insights and frames of thought have not been done to answer these questions; many studies of this general area stray far from the *interpersonal* focus they should have.

In order to show how Sullivan's points of view might have been applied to these problems, we shall, however, assume that such studies were done and that they revealed the following *anxieties in white people:* Blacks are less intelligent than whites and will drag down the academic level of any school in which they form a sizable number.

(2) Blacks are less industrious, less punctual, and less reliable than whites. Schools must adjust their standards to the maximums they can demand of their students, and schools will therefore be able to demand

less of their students, both in academic excellence and general deportment, if the schools contain large numbers of blacks.

(3) Blacks are sexually more licentious and promiscuous than whites and will cause a deterioration of sexual mores in any school which they attend in large numbers.

(4) Blacks have higher incidences of lying, stealing, illicit drug usage, and physical violence than whites, and will cause a lowering of morality in schools they attend. They will drag white students down with them.

Assuming that *participant observer* investigators have established that these are some of the main anxieties of whites about blacks, the next question, from a Sullivanian point of view, is: What security operations are whites employing to protect themselves from feeling these painful anxieties? In other words, what interpersonal acts and attitudes do the whites use to avoid the emotional pain they would feel if they intermingled with blacks or frankly faced their reasons for not wanting to intermingle with them?

A major, obvious security operation of whites is physical separation of themselves from blacks in all socially practical ways. They live apart from them, work separately, and carry out their social activities independently. Black segregation is not the primary problem. The basic problem is that, in protecting themselves against their anxieties about blacks, the whites segregate themselves. Black segregation is a result of white self-segregation.

Other white security operations involve things they do and say to justify their self-segregation. They state

repeatedly that blacks are less intelligent, less moral, less punctual, less reliable, less prudent, and less industrious than whites, and they cite anecdotes to bolster these statements. Using the security operation of selective inattention, experiences with honest, reliable, morally conforming blacks are disregarded, while stories about undesirable blacks are exchanged among whites.

Another white security operation is to dehumanize blacks. "They're different than we are." "Black women don't suffer as white women do when they have babies; black women have them in an animallike way." "They don't feel things the way we do." "They are only two hundred and fifty years removed from barbaric African tribalism." Educational campaigns and slowly changing social patterns have had an impact on white opinions in recent decades, but dehumanizing blacks by categorizing them as imperfectly civilized or animalistic is still a common white security operation, especially among lower middle class and laboring class groups.

By such security operations whites protect themselves from their anxieties about blacks and justify their self-segregation from them, and school segregation accompanies group segregation.

In the same way in which it paralyzes communication between two persons, anxiety paralyzes communication between two groups. Because of their anxieties about blacks, whites cannot communicate freely with them when opportunities to do so occur, and because of their anxieties blacks similarly cannot communicate well with whites. The interpersonal tensions between blacks and whites hence continue un-

resolved, and white anxieties remain strong. Anxiety and paralyzed communication reinforce each other in a vicious crcle.

Improved communication would, of course, require knowledge of the anxieties of blacks in regard to whites; however, to simplify this presentation we shall not consider that aspect of the problem, since our object is to show how Sullivan's concepts can be applied to social group problems and not to examine black-white racial difficulties exhaustively.

The next step in applying Sullivan's principles is to bring the whites' anxieties about blacks into their focus of awareness, and to explore these anxieties. Most whites have only vague concepts of the extent and strength of their antiblack feelings. They are even more unaware of how their antiblack attitudes and actions are security operations to help them cope with their marked anxieties about blacks.

Whites must become aware of the ways in which they disguise from themselves their antiblack anxieties and their security operations in regard to these anxieties. For example, the well-meaning Southern Baptist who justifies church segregation by saying, "Blacks feel better, and can worship better, when they stay with their own kind," must become *aware* that his attitude is a security operation to camouflage from himself his profound emotional discomforts about closeness to blacks. To paraphrase Sullivan, much that is unaware must be formulated and communicated. In group discussions, long-term public educational campaigns, seminars in vocational and social settings, and many other kinds of interchanges whites gradually can become *aware* of their anxieties about blacks and the

ways in which they protect themselves against these anxieties.

Most programs and campaigns to change white attitudes have failed because they have concentrated on telling whites what they *should* do and feel about blacks. Such campaigns will be successful only when they bring into whites' awareness their fears, dreads, and panic, and deal with them. Then white people will move forward because they *can* do so.

The anxieties of the whites must be dealt with extensively and repeatedly. They must be reassured in all realistic ways of the groundlessness of their fears. They must see that statistics which tend to support their fears (high rates of crime and drug abuse in black inner city districts) are the results of segregation and not the products of racial defects in blacks; they must see how these things are caused by the segregation of blacks in socially deprived neighborhoods, exclusion from good jobs and adequate housing, and many other factors. Most of all, they must comprehend that black segregation is basically the result of white self-segregation away from them.

A long process of social consensual validation begins, involving both whites and blacks. The anxieties and the security operations of whites, and the anxieties and security operations of blacks, are slowly dealt with in ever widening discussions and public educational campaigns making use of school groups, work groups, professional groups, religious groups, other social groups, and the entire spectrum of news and public information media. Resolution of the whites', as well as the blacks', anxieties and security operations proceeds gradually in a general process of social consensual val-

idation. Social psychotherapy thus moves along the same lines as individual psychotherapy.

Once this process is well under way it should be accompanied by large numbers of interpersonal experiences involving the two groups in many kinds of social situations and discussion programs. Such experiences must at first be deliberately planned, and emphasis should be placed on allaying the anxieties of both groups. In this context school desegregation is facilitated, and the schools in turn provide situations for interaction in which consensual validation and social reassurance for the whites can occur.

As white and black anxieties and security operations are resolved, as hidden feelings are brought into full focuses of awareness, and consensual validations are gradually achieved, Sullivan's principle of the tendency toward health begins to operate. That is, as the psychological barriers that keep whites and blacks apart are dissolved the two groups begin to associate more. Blacks filter into white schools and neighborhoods, job equality is achieved, and social intermingling proceeds in natural ways. *Once the obstacles created by social sickness are removed society grows spontaneously toward health.*

Sullivan's *one-genus postulate*, that *we are all much more simply human than otherwise*, is obvious in its application to racial difficulties.


## GENERATION GAP PROBLEMS

The term "generation gap problems" will be employed here to designate a broad spectrum of interper-

251

sonal difficulties between adolescents and young adults on one hand, and their parents and general adult society on the other.

Generation gap problems include both intrafamilial problems between parents and their adolescent and young adult children, and public conflicts of young people with administrative adults who are two decades or more older than they. This latter category embraces conflicts between university administrators and student groups, clashes of law enforcement officials with youths, and many similar difficulties. In the following discussion adolescents and young adults will often be collectively referred to by the term "youths," and the older generations by the term "adults."

Generation gap problems assume various forms in different decades. In the 1930's, much influenced by the rigors of a severe economic depression, generation gap difficulties were muted; public clashes were rare and parent-youth conflicts were to a considerable degree suppressed by stark economic necessities as well as ingrained customs and attitudes. In the 1960's generation gap problems were open and strident; discord between parents and youths, and public strife between youths on one hand and university officials, law enforcement officers, and public officials on the other, were common. In the 1970's the two groups have tended simply to go their separate ways, with characteristic beliefs, life-styles, and customs of their own; public collisions have been uncommon and parent-youth clashes have tended to be concealed more than in the 1960's.

Sullivan's methods can be applied to evaluating and resolving generation gap problems in both familial and general social situations.

252

The principle of *participant observation* is first employed. Ideally, members of each group participate alertly in activities with the other group, observing their feelings, attitudes, and customs; both adults and youths in deliberate, planned ways examine the opposing group. However, in practical terms the adults must in most cases initiate and carry out such participant observation. The youths as a rule are too apprehensive about censure, rejection, or domination by adults to make initial participant observation on their part workable; they tend to abandon it at the first signs of tension or conflict, and defensively shrink back.

Hence our discussion will be directed mainly toward adults, outlining how they may proceed as participant observers with youths.

Most adults, especially middle-aged ones, know little about what goes on in the youth culture. They may not know the names, let alone the characteristics, of pop singers, writers, film stars, and pundits whom the youths consider eminent. The differences between the two groups in reading preferences, music tastes, recreational patterns, food selections, choices of intoxicants (marijuana versus alcohol), religious concepts, clothing, body ornaments, and many other things often are marked; each group has little comprehension of the life-style of the other, or sees it only in caricatured ways.

The general cultural knowledge of the two groups (Shakespeare and Dickens versus Rilke and Hesse, Zen and Hindu mysticism versus conventional Western religions) is quite different. The adults feel that the youths are ignorant and badly educated, and the youths feel that the cultural knowledge of the adults is irrelevant to modern needs. The youths accuse adults

of adhering to outmoded literature, music, and customs because of snobbism and sham, and the adults accuse the youths of grasping at each passing fad.

In their participant observation activities with youths adults must work hard to put aside censorious, belittling attitudes. Participant observation is fruitful only when it is carried out uncritically. The partipant observer's aim is to learn what the other party feels, thinks, and does. Censure quickly clouds an observer's view, and it is quickly sensed by the other party, who decamps. If a psychotherapist were to scold his patients he soon would have none; social participant observation operates similarly. Sullivan, as noted, said that psychotherapy was the hardest work he knew and there was no fun in it; participant observation in solving a generation gap problem is equally hard work and, at first, there is little fun in it. The alternative to such work, however, is to allow the generation gap to widen, with all the dangers and loneliness that this brings.

Adults often find their efforts to span the generation gap exasperating and seemingly fruitless. However, the adult who understands his role as a participant observer will do his work effectively, and perhaps in time with pleasure. People often take vacations abroad to observe foreign cultures; it can be pleasurable to study a foreign culture in one's own home.

In most cases adolescents and young adults accept the efforts of older adults as participant observers after an initial period of jeering skepticism. In fact, most youths have a deep sense of isolation and are hungry for closeness with adults. Many sociological and psychiatric studies of youths indicate that they yearn for a

loser family life and better relationships with their parents. Most of them state, in response to question-naires, that looseness of family life was a major defect of their formative years. Nevertheless, most youths at first feel that adult attempts to get close to them are merely maneuvers to change their viewpoints and dominate them. As a rule this suspiciousness quickly decreases if adults candidly outline what they are do-ing and what their objects are. Though the youths in the beginning are doubtful that adults can set aside their prejudices and viewpoints sufficiently to be true participant observers, they usually give them A's for effort.

All participant observation is inevitably a two-way process no matter how skeptical or hesitant one side may be, and in time the youths learn a good deal about the adults. In the process they develop greater under-standing and more tolerance, albeit condescending at times, of the adults' points of view, and the youths' viewpoints and customs are always affected to some degree by such understanding. Ideally the youths should become as active in participant observation as the adults, but this rarely occurs; the preponderance of work in spanning a generation gap must be done by the adults.

The next step, using Sullivan's principles,    to ask: What are the *anxieties* of the youths that cause them to isolate themselves from the adults? Many psychiatric studies answer this question.

The youths are apprehensive that each close contact with adults will result in:

(1) Insensitive domination of them by adults.

(2) Persuasion of them to accept adult viewpoints

and customs which they feel are hypocritical and false.

(3) Loss of their individuality and their personal and group identity.

(4) Censure and depreciation of them by the adults, no matter how well-intentioned the adults may be in the beginning, with consequent deterioration of the adult-youth relationship.

(5) Painful rejection of the youths by the adults and abandonment by them.

The next step, following Sullivan's format, is to ask: What are the major security operations which the youths employ to protect themselves against awareness of their anxieties, and the distress they would feel if they moved closer toward the adults?

A main, obvious security operation is to isolate themselves from adults so that domination, depreciation, and rejection of them by adults cannot occur. Despite protests that they are indifferent to what adults feel about them, most youths are extremely sensitive about the attitudes of their parents and adult social authorities.

Adolescents and young adults often adopt clothing fashions, grooming modes, language, sexual behavior, and other life-style manners which increase the distance between them and adults. Although these customs have multiple determinants, a major motivation is the youths' need to increase their distance from adults by strident nonconformance to adult manners and beliefs. In short, a wide variety of security operations are incorporated into these aspects of the youths' life-styles, since markedly different clothing, hair styles, footgear, body ornaments, and customs constitute, among other things, ways of repelling adults, who find such things puzzling and disgusting.

Similarly, the habitual use of lewd sexual terms is not simply a franker means of speech, as the youths proclaim; it also functions as a security operation since it repels adults, and the youths thus avoid closeness with them and the anxieties this would arouse. Likewise, by flaunting sexual behavior that adults find unacceptable, the youths keep themselves distant from adults.

In still another security operation, adolescents and young adults frequently maintain that their life-style, in addition to being different from that of adults, is superior to it. They state that they are not hypocritical, artificial, unhealthily restrained, snobbish and materialistic, as they claim the adults are. Such an attitude enables them to overlook defects in their own viewpoints and activities, and they thus avoid the anxiety that such self-scrutiny would occasion. Moreover, they can justify their distance from adults, since closeness to adults can be decried as a compromise with the adults' false sets of values.

The youth culture's interest in Oriental religions and other mystical beliefs is more than a search for new faiths to replace lost old ones; it reassures the youths that they will not be reabsorbed in time into the adults' way of life. A final security operation of youths consists of angry confrontations with adult institutions, with their occasional public violence. In essence the youths say: It is not you who censure and reject us, but we who censure and reject you. It is your ways and beliefs that are corrupt and rotten, not ours.

The next step in resolving a generation gap problem through the use of Sullivan's guidelines is to help the youths become aware of the basic anxieties and security operations that cause them to withdraw from adults.

This requires the utmost ingenuity and patience, and it can be accomplished only if the adolescents and young adults are strongly reassured at every step. In essence, the adults must say frequently and emphatically: We do not want to dominate you, to convert you to our ways, or to deprive you of your personal and group identity. We want to know you, and we want you to know us. We want a comfortable closeness with you in which easy two-way communication can occur. If it can be achieved, such closeness and communication will be healthier for all of us. The youths at first will feel that such reassurances are only ploys; these reassurances must be given often and strongly both in words and deeds to assuage the anxiousness that closeness with adults arouses in them.

Nonverbal factors usually are more important than verbal ones in adult-youth encounters. The unspoken dialogue carries far more weight than the spoken one. The fact that the adults and the youths come together, do things together, talk, and go away, and that the youths still have the same viewpoints, grooming style, and clothing fashions that they had, often makes a greater impression than what was said. That the adults make no attempt to alter the customs and attitudes to which the youths cling constitutes the major reassurance the adults give.

This is a crucial Sullivanian point. The primary goal is interpersonal closeness and comfortable, anxiety-free communication. A familial or social adult-youth conflict will gradually be resolved if this aim is accomplished.

Any direct, deliberate attempt to change the youths is fatal. If the essentially psychotherapeutic nature of

the adult-youth encounter is forgotten, and if the adults attempt to persuade the youths to alter their life-styles and beliefs, the fears of the youths are confirmed and their anxieties about closeness to adults are doubled. They become alarmed that, under the guise of dialogue, the adults are trying to dominate them, to quash their individuality, and to induce them to accept the adults' views and patterns of living. They feel that censure is implied by these adult actions, and that rejection of them by the adults is inevitable if they do not knuckle under. They break off the dialogue and flee.

When adult-youth interaction is successful, the youths of course learn a good deal about the adults. They get at least limited concepts of what the adults' anxieties and security operations are ("Man, you should see how hungup they are and how they keep ripping themselves off all the time"). With understanding comes compassion; people usually have little fear of those for whom they feel sorry. (As noted before, we are discussing generation gap problems only in terms of the youths' anxieties and the adults' roles as participant observers, since our primary aim is not to discuss generation gap diffiulties but to illustrate the use of Sullivan's principles in solving broader interpersonal problems).

Over a period of time, which may be months or years depending on the problems attacked and the goals sought, consensual validation between the youths and adults occurs. It comes piecemeal; there are many benefits for both sides as partial degrees of consensual validation are achieved.

As consensual validation is gradually accomplished,

Sullivan's principle of the tendency toward health comes into play. As the barriers between the two groups come down they spontaneously draw together. Interpersonal and emotional closeness develops; this occurs when the process is occurring between parents and children in a family, or between administration and students in a university, or in any other setting.

Thus, Sullivan's one-genus postulate, that we are all much more simply human than otherwise, finds justification. Each side finds the other more reasonable, appealing, and likable than they had ever imagined they could be. If the adults and youths know what they are driving at, in the explicit terms of the one-genus postulate, they are more likely to find it.

## GENERAL CONSIDERATIONS IN USING SULLIVAN'S PRINCIPLES FOR SOLVING SOCIAL PROBLEMS

Sullivan's approach to psychiatry lends itself to the solution of social group problems more effectively than any other major psychiatric point of view. It does so because it was developed in interpersonal settings and is expressed in interpersonal terms.

This fact becomes obvious when Sullivan's system is compared with other psychiatric theories. For example, when any other form of behavior theory (Skinner's operant conditioning, Watson's behaviorism, behavior therapy approaches, learning theory, and others) employed to interpret and mold social forces it usually is cold, mechanical, and stringently dogmatic; at its worst, it is coercive. This is what has happened in the Soviet Union and its dependent countries where be-

havior theory, based on Pavlov's neurophysiological experiments on animals and combined with the Marxist doctrines of intellectual materialism and economic determinism, is the official form of psychology. Communication theory and general systems theory, despite promise shown in their early stages of development, have not evolved sufficiently to be fruitful in solving specific social difficulties. Communication theory relies too heavily on conscious, verbal interchanges and does not adequately take human anxieties and passions into account. General systems theory, in addition to its vagueness, suffers from the same defects.

Freudian psychoanalysis, with its emphases on intrapsychic machinery (id, ego, superego, and other devices), infantile sexuality, and dream analysis can be applied to social problems only by contorting it out of its true shape and borrowing many features from interpersonal psychiatry. Jungian theory, with its reliance on concepts of inherited mental patterns (archetypes) and the collective (racial) unconscious, can be used to interpret past history, especially ancient civilizations. However, it is too highly speculative and imprecise for application to current problems; it also lends itself too strongly to spiritual and mystical interpretations of human dilemmas. Other psychiatric systems such as existential theory, Adlerian viewpoints, Gestalt theory, and many others have not been elaborated in sufficient detail to provide useful ways for evaluating and solving social problems.

Sullivan, in contrast with almost all other psychiatric pioneers, developed his ideas in *group* settings; he evolved his basic concepts while working with groups on the wards of psychiatric hospitals, rather than

while doing individual psychotherapy with single patients in consultation rooms. Moreover, from the beginning of his career he viewed a psychiatric ward as merely a special kind of *social* situation for people who were struggling to solve special kinds of interpersonal and emotional problems. He formed his system of thought by participating in the ongoing interpersonal relationships between the patients and the staff, and by observing what went on among the patients themselves. Sullivan first used the word "interpersonal" in 1926, when he had been in psychiatry for four years, and at about the same time he first employed the word "social" in talking about psychiatric disturbances. Virtually all other pioneers in psychological approaches to psychiatric illnesses worked in one-to-one psychotherapy with individual patients, and their viewpoints strongly reflect this fact.

In brief, Sullivan's concepts have unique usefulness in evaluating and solving the problems of social groups since they were developed in the contexts of social settings and are expressed in interpersonal terms.

The various Sullivanian principles which were employed in the illustrations of the first two sections of this chapter may be listed and summarized, in the order of their usage, as follows:

1. *Participant Observation.* The person who undertakes to ameliorate a social group difficulty participates in the activities and discussions of the group, or groups, involved, both as a means of observing their needs and feelings and as a way of getting the information he requires for subsequent steps.

2. *Anxiety and Security Operations.* The group members' *anxieties* (painful emotional forces) which

are causing the social conflict are identified, and the security operations by which they protect themselves from feeling the discomfort of their anxieties are investigated.

3. *Awareness.* These anxieties and security operations are brought into clear focuses of awareness by the use of many forms of individual and group discussions, public interchanges, general information, and educational programs, and other communicative processes. The utmost flexibility and ingenuity must be employed, fitting techniques in each case to the problems of the particular situation

4. *Consensual Validation.* Through long-term, multifaceted evaluations, discussions, and interactions, the group members achieve consensual validation; they arrive at consensuses of feeling and thinking with one another and validate them in repeated interpersonal experiences. They do this both with members of their own group and with members of the group with whom they are in conflict, or from whom they are alienated. Healthier, freer, more comfortable interaction develops. The anxieties and security operations which had paralyzed communication between the two groups are resolved.

5. *The Tendency Toward Health.* As interpersonal barriers are removed the members of the clashing groups spontaneously develop close, harmonious relationships with one another. Sullivanian theory maintains that there is an innate tendency toward health when the causes of social conflict and estrangement are removed.

6. *The One-Genus Postulate.* The increased understanding, interest, and compassion of the two groups

in regard to each other exemplify Sullivan's one-genus postulate, that we are all much more simply human than otherwise.

In addition, others of Sullivan's concepts can be utilized in solving social group difficulties. The principle of reciprocal emotions and the concept of dynamisms (Chapter 3) may be useful. Sullivan's four-part investigative approach, consisting of the inception, the reconnaissance, the detailed inquiry, and the termination, or interruption, provides a convenient format for evaluating a problem. Other Sullivanian principles and procedures can be used in lesser ways.

In actual practice, of course, the various stages of solving a social problem would overlap considerably. Several stages would be going on at the same time, and backtracking and repetition would be necessary in endlessly flexible ways. Moreover, different sections of the groups would be in diverse phases at any one time.

There is a limiting factor in the application of Sullivanian principles to the solution of social problems. They can be used only in a free society. Each person must be at liberty to explore all aspects of his interpersonal situations and to express himself without fear or restraint. If limits are put on what can be asked and said, and the extent to which viewpoints can be discussed in all kinds of information media, these methods will not work. If attempts were made to use Sullivan's principles in societies in which restraints on expression existed, the process would quickly deteriorate into a campaign of propaganda, brainwashing, and social coercion by one group against another.

In the broadest sense, there is a distinctly American imprint on Sullivan's thought. He reflects the aspira-

tions, if not the full reality, of his culture. He conveys the feeling that, given enough freedom, work, and time, most social difficulties can be solved. The key word is *problem,* which implies that a solution is both possible and expected. He feels that his concepts can be applied to neighborhood conflicts, employer-employee disputes, ethnic clashes, religious estrangements, political antagonisms, and other social difficulties.

Sullivan practiced what he preached. In his writings and actions he fought against racial discrimination, legal injustices, social blights, and economic deprivations. There is, perhaps, something symbolic in the fact that by his expressed desire he was buried in Arlington National Cemetery.

# A Selected Descriptive Bibliography
of Sullivan's Works

SULLIVAN'S work appears in seven easily available volumes, which vary much in quality and nature. We shall discuss them in the order of their possible interest to readers rather than by their successive years of publication. The first six of these books are available in paperback editions.

*The Psychiatric Interview,* New York, W. W. Norton, 1954, 246 pages. The material of this book is drawn mainly from recordings of a lecture series which Sullivan gave in 1944, and repeated in 1945. Although it deals mainly with psychiatric evaluation of patients it also contains a clear presentation of Sullivan's interpersonal approach to psychiatry. It is the best-written, most lucid, and shortest of Sullivan's books. Some parts, however, are poor. The section which outlines steps for taking a patient's life history and evaluating his current interpersonal adjustment is trite, and all of Chapter 8 on diagnostic signs and descriptions of psychiatric disorders is weak. The thirteen-page introduction by Otto Allen Will is excellent. Anyone reading Sullivan for the first time should begin with this book.

*The Interpersonal Theory of Psychiatry,* New York, W. W. Norton, 1953, 393 pages. This book contains the last complete series of lectures Sullivan gave. It begins with an

outline of his general points of view and proceeds into a very detailed account of his concepts of personality development from infancy through late adolescence. It ends with short sections on schizophrenia, paranoid disorders, and a few other topics. The eight-page introduction by Mabel Blake Cohen is good.

Like much of Sullivan's writing, extensive sections of this book are poorly organized and difficult to read. It demands careful study by a reader who already has some knowledge of Sullivan's terminology and concepts. Understanding it is facilitated by reading with ball-point pen in hand for underlining definitions and important statements to which later references can be made when obscure passages are encountered. The reader unfortunately must do the work that better editing would have accomplished.

*Clinical Studies in Psychiatry*, New York, W. W. Norton, 1956, 386 pages. This volume is made up of selections from seminars and lectures which Sullivan gave to the staff of the Chestnut Lodge private psychiatric hospital in Rockville, Maryland, five years before he died. It is the most comprehensive presentation Sullivan made of his views on the nature and causes of psychiatric disorders. About half the book is devoted to schizophrenia, paranoid disorders, and obsessive neuroses, the conditions Sullivan studied most extensively. Some other psychiatric disorders and various general aspects of psychiatric illnesses are covered. The book is quite uneven in quality and literary style. It assumes that the reader is well grounded in clinical psychiatry and has had experience in treating psychiatric patients.

*Conceptions of Modern Psychiatry*, New York, W. W. Norton, 1953, 298 pages. This is a reedition of the only volume of Sullivan's work that appeared during his lifetime. It is composed of five lectures which he delivered in 1939. In later years Sullivan stated that the first three lectures no longer represented his mature views. Much of the fourth

lecture is rambling and commonplace. The fifth lecture, on psychotherapy, is by far the best. The book ends with a fifty-five-page well-written commentary on Sullivan's theories by Patrick Mullahy, which covers a few topics that are clearly presented nowhere else in Sullivan's works.

The four volumes listed above were the only ones planned by the committee on Sullivan's writings which was formed after his death. However, three more volumes were later published. They contain some of Sullivan's early, unimportant articles and miscellaneous items from his later years. These three volumes are listed below.

*Schizophrenia as a Human Process*, New York, W. W. Norton, 1962, 363 pages. This book contains thirteen articles which Sullivan published in psychiatric journals and other periodicals between 1924 and 1935, mainly on schizophrenia. It ends with a brief excerpt from the book *Personal Psychopathology* (described below). Many of these articles are tedious and banal, and others represent Sullivan's first, fumbling efforts to formulate his ideas. Only one of them, the fifteen-page article titled "Socio-Psychiatric Research," is outstanding. In it Sullivan describes in a pithy, brilliant way his work with schizophrenics on his special ward at the Sheppard and Enoch Pratt Hospital, and the conclusions he drew from it.

*The Fusion of Psychiatry and Social Science*, New York, W. W. Norton, 1964, 364 pages. Seventeen articles which Sullivan wrote between 1934 and his death in 1949 are drawn together to form this book. Some of them are unsigned editorials from the journal *Psychiatry*, of which Sullivan was for many years the editor. Most of these articles are unimportant and badly dated. Three, however, are excellent; they are "The Data of Psychiatry," "The Illusion of Personal Individuality," and "The Meaning of Anxiety in

Psychiatry and Life." This book fails in its attempt to portray Sullivan as a major contributor to modern sociology, for he was not.

*Personal Psychopathology,* New York, W. W. Norton, 1972, 390 pages. Sullivan began this book in 1929, when he had been in psychiatry for only seven years, and worked no more on it after 1933. He decided definitely against publishing it in 1933 and afterward stated he had greatly altered his views about many things that were in it. The manuscript unfortunately survived him and, much against the judgment of many of his colleagues, was published twenty-three years after his death. It is a rambling, eccentric, passionate book which is clearly autobiographical in parts. This book has no general psychiatric value. It can be of use only to persons who are making detailed studies of Sullivan's painful evolution toward the emotional and intellectual maturity he achieved late in life.

# Index

## A

Aberdeen Proving Ground, 65
Adler, Alfred, 39, 73
Adolescence, Personality development in, Sullivan's views on, 144–45, 182–89; early, 182–87; late, 187–89
American dilemmas, current, relevance of, Sullivan's psychiatry applied to, 243–65; generation gap problems, 251–60; racial problems, 243–51; social problems, 260–65
*American Journal of Psychiatry,* 43
American Psychiatric Museum Association, 18 *n.*
Amsterdam, Holland, 67, 241
Anxiety, Sullivan's concept of, 78–86, 95, 125, 262–63; awareness caused by, 108; in psychotherapy, 210–16; in white people, 246–51; in youth, 255–56
Anxiety-producing father, 163
Anxiety-producing mother, 153, 155–57
Anxiety-producing nipple, 148, 149–53

Anxiety-ridden me, 157, 158–59
Arlington National Cemetery, 67, 265
"As if" security operation, 92, 96
Atomic bomb, 65
Awareness, 108, 263; unawareness and, Sullivan's concept of, 98–109

## B

Bagehot, Walter, 29
Baltimore, Maryland, 42–49, 53
Bethesda, Maryland, 61
Brill, Abraham A., 57
Burnham, Donald, L., 18 *n.*

## C

Chance, role of, in personality development, 88–89
Chapman, A. H., preface by, 11–15
Chapman, Ross McClure, 45
Chestnut Lodge, Rockville, Maryland, 65, 268

*274*

*275*

Ithaca, New York, 24

## J

Johns Hopkins Medical School, 39, 40, 52, 116
Johnson, Charles S., 60
Jung, Carl, 28, 39, 73, 98, 105
Juvenile period, personality development in, Sullivan's views on, 144, 175–82; preadolescence, 179–82; social group as a therapeutic force, 175–79

## K

Kempf, Edward J., 41–42

## L

Language, role of, in consensual validation and syntaxic thinking, 171–72, 173
Latency period of personality development, 176
Learning as interpersonal process, 172–74
Levy, David, 44
Life-style, of youth, 257; Sullivan's, 61–62
Loneliness, 173
Loyola University School of Medicine, 31, 32
Lust, Sullivan's approach to, 135–36, 138, 139, 183, 184; as an integrating force, 185–87

## M

Malinowski, Bronislaw, 44
Malok, Johann, 30
McDougal, William, 44
Mead, George Herbert, 44, 94
Mental health professional workers, role of, basic, 111, 114–15
Meyer, Adolf, 39–41, 44
Moore, Thomas V., 44, 116–17
Mother-child relationship, 163–64
Mother concepts, infant's, anxiety-producing, 153, 154; emotionally comfortable, 153–55; fusion of, 155–57
Mullahy, Patrick, 57, 269

## N

Nashville, Tennessee, 60
National Association for the Advancement of Colored People (NAACP), 60
Needs, 128–31
Neuroses, 40
Newton, Isaac, 132
New York City, 52–60, 61
Noble, Douglas, 18 n.
Noninterpersonal introspection, Sullivan's objection to, 230, 233–34
Norwich, New York, 18–19, 21

## O

Objects, infant's first concepts of, Sullivan's views of, 147–53; anxiety-producing nipple, 148, 149–53; emotionally comfortable nipple, 148, 149–53

279

r'